T0219581

Introducing Algorithms in C

A Step by Step Guide
to Algorithms in C

Luciano Manelli

Apress®

Introducing Algorithms in C: A Step by Step Guide to Algorithms in C

Luciano Manelli
Taranto, Italy

ISBN-13 (pbk): 978-1-4842-5622-0   ISBN-13 (electronic): 978-1-4842-5623-7
https://doi.org/10.1007/978-1-4842-5623-7

Managing Director, Apress Media LLC: Welmoed Spahr
Acquisitions Editor: Steve Anglin
Development Editor: Matthew Moodie
Coordinating Editor: Mark Powers

Cover designed by eStudioCalamar

Cover image designed by Freepik (www.freepik.com)

Distributed to the book trade worldwide by Apress Media, LLC, 1 New York Plaza, New York, NY 10004, U.S.A. Phone 1-800-SPRINGER, fax (201) 348-4505, e-mail orders-ny@springer-sbm.com, or visit www.springeronline.com. Apress Media, LLC is a California LLC and the sole member (owner) is Springer Science + Business Media Finance Inc (SSBM Finance Inc). SSBM Finance Inc is a **Delaware** corporation.

For information on translations, please e-mail editorial@apress.com; for reprint, paperback, or audio rights, please email bookpermissions@springernature.com.

Apress titles may be purchased in bulk for academic, corporate, or promotional use. eBook versions and licenses are also available for most titles. For more information, reference our Print and eBook Bulk Sales web page at www.apress.com/bulk-sales.

Any source code or other supplementary material referenced by the author in this book is available to readers on GitHub via the book's product page, located at www.apress.com/9781484256220. For more detailed information, please visit www.apress.com/source-code.

Printed on acid-free paper

To my daughter, Sara

To my son, Marco

To my mum, Anna

Table of Contents

About the Author

 **Luciano Manelli** was born in Taranto (Italy), where he currently resides with his family. He graduated in electronic engineering at the Polytechnic of Bari at 24 years of age, and then he served as an officer in the Navy. In 2012, he received a PhD in computer science from the Department of Informatics, University of Bari Aldo Moro.

He is a contract professor at the Polytechnic of Bari and at the University of Bari Aldo Moro. He is a professionally certified engineer, an innovation manager, and the author of several IT technical books for different publishers. In 2014 he started working for the Port Network Authority of the Ionian Sea – Port of Taranto, after working for 13 years for InfoCamere SCpA as a software developer.

You can find out more at his LinkedIn page: `it.linkedin.com/in/lucianomanelli`.

About the Technical Reviewer

 **Michael Thomas** has worked in software development for more than 20 years as an individual contributor, team lead, program manager, and vice president of engineering. Michael has more than 10 years of experience working with mobile devices. His current focus is in the medical sector, using mobile devices to accelerate information transfer between patients and healthcare providers.

Introduction

This book serves as a starting point for anyone who is beginning their study of computer science and information systems. Algorithms play an important role in programming, and they can be considered the cornerstone of computer science, because computer programs would not exist without algorithms. In fact, understanding a problem and getting a solution is a fundamental condition for software development and problem-solving strategies. Therefore, the aim of this book is to explain algorithms in different ways and then teach you how to analyze new algorithms. In this book, we will use the C language to verify the correctness of the algorithms.

Chapter 1 introduces data types (simple and structured), and Chapter 2 defines the algorithms and flowcharts with graphical and textual explanations. We'll look at simple and complex standard algorithms, as well as their flowcharts. Everything is integrated with explanations, schemas, and tables to show the step-by-step evolution of the algorithms.

The main analyzed algorithms are the following: the sum of three or n numbers in a loop, the decimal to binary conversion, the maximum and minimum search, the linear/sequential search, the binary search, the bubble sort, the selection sort, the merging of two sorted arrays, and the reading chars from file algorithm, stack management, and the recursive algorithm (factorial and Fibonacci sequence).

The last chapter is devoted to the introduction of the C language and the implementation of code related to the algorithms in this book. Many C programs are explained.

CHAPTER 1

Data Structures

The study of algorithms is connected to data structures. A *data structure* is a way to store data to facilitate organization and modifications. Every data structure is used for a specific purpose, so it is important to know the characteristics of several of them so you can choose the data structures that are appropriate for the operations performed by an algorithm.

Variables and Constants

A *variable* represents a memory location that stores an assigned value. Each variable is associated with a data type and stores one or some values. Variables can change their value during program execution, but they cannot change their structure or their data type. A variable is characterized by three elements.

- **Name**: A variable's name must be unique and inherent to the programming context, mainly to avoid ambiguity in the program.

- **Type**: A variable's type indicates whether the variable is an integer, a float, a character, and so on. Each type allocates different space in central memory.

- **Content**: A variable's content is the value assigned to the variable in a step of the program execution.

© Luciano Manelli 2020
L. Manelli, *Introducing Algorithms in C*, https://doi.org/10.1007/978-1-4842-5623-7_1

Furthermore, the most important operators are assignment and comparison.

- **Assignment**: The symbol = (a single equal sign) assigns a value to a variable.

- **Test for equality**: The symbol == (two equal signs) compares the values of two variables (an expression with a final value of true or false).

For example, if we wanted to assign the value 4 to the variable a and the value 5 to the variable b, we would write the following:

```
a=4;
b=5;
```

For example, if we wanted to compare a and b, we would write the following:

```
a==b;
```

Note that C and Java programs use this notation.

For example, if we wanted to sum two variables (a and b) and we wanted to store the result of this operation in the variable SUM, we would write the following:

```
SUM = a+b;
```

In some cases, we might be interested in the iterative sum of a set of values for an algorithm. For example, if we wanted to know the sum of some integer values, we could use an intermediate variable and write the following:

```
intermediate_sum = final_sum + new_value;
final_sum = intermediate_sum;
```

We could also write in a compact form, without using an intermediate variable, as shown here:

```
final_sum = final_sum + new_value;
```

In computer science, we can add the new_value to the content of the variable final_sum and store the result in the same variable, final_sum. Reading the formula from left to right, the first variable final_sum indicates the new value of the sum, the second variable indicates the value currently stored in the variable final_sum, and the third variable indicates a new value (new_value) that has to be added to the current variable final_sum.

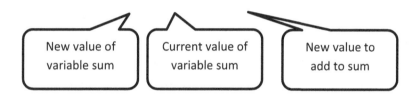

In some cases, we are interested in the use of a counter, such as an index i that increases its value at each step of an algorithm. For example, consider an integer index named i that is incremented by 1 at each step. This condition is expressed in the following formula:

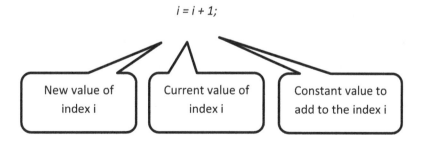

Reading the formula from left to right, the first index i indicates the new value of the counter, the second variable indicates the value currently stored in the counter i, and the third variable indicates a new value (1) that has to be added to the current variable i.

Constants are similar to variables, but they cannot change their value during program execution. They also usually have a different type of declaration in the program. For example, if we wanted to assign an integer value (4) to the constant const in the C language, we would write the following:

```
#define CONST = 4
```

Once a constant is defined, it cannot be modified by the program.

Primitive Types

It is possible to define the following primitive types:

- **Numeric**: This type includes integers (numbers without decimal points) and floats (numbers with a decimal after a decimal point). They are stored differently in memory and have different scopes. A float is usually declared when more precision is needed.

- **Character**: The character type includes letters and dots.

- **Boolean (true and false)**: Booleans usually are used to compare variable values. The comparison can be either true or false.

Structured Types

To represent data in other ways, it is possible to define structured types. The following are the basic structuring methods presented in this chapter:

- Array

- Linked list

- Queue

- Stack

- Graph

- Tree

- Hash table

- Record

- File

Array

One of the most important elementary data structures is the array. An *array* is a sequence of n items of the same data type stored contiguously in computer memory. An array is accessible by specifying a value of the array's index (an integer between 0 and n – 1, where n is the length of the array).

So, an array is characterized by the following:

- Name (for example, a)

- Length (n)

- Elements of the array accessible by index i

5

For example, to create an array a of six integer elements (4, 1, 34, 56, 7, 0), we would write the following:

```
a (0) = 4;
a (1) = 1;
a (2) = 34;
a (3) = 56;
a (4) = 7;
a (5) = 0;
```

In graphical form, we would write it as follows :

4	1	34	56	7	0
i=0	i=1	i=2	i=3	i=4	i=5

Arrays are used to implement a variety of other data structures. The most important is the *string*, a sequence of characters from the alphabet (for example, the word *Luciano* is a string of seven characters). Furthermore, it is possible to combine arrays and define multidimensional arrays (in other words, matrixes). Each element of an array can be accessed in the same amount of time, and this feature distinguishes arrays from linked lists, discussed next.

Linked Lists

Another important elementary data structure is the *linked list* (a one-dimensional, or singly linked, list). A linked list is a data structure in which the elements are arranged in a sequence of zero or more elements called *nodes*. Each element contains two kinds of information.

- **Data (or key)**: The value.

- **Pointer**: The variable that stores the address where another node of the list resides, in other words, a link to another node of the linked list (i.e., $L_2 = \text{next}[L_1]$). If there is no successor of a node, a special pointer called *null* (or *NIL*) is used (i.e., $\text{next}[L_3]$= null, or NIL). Except the last one, each node contains a single pointer to the next element. Figure 1-1 illustrates this.

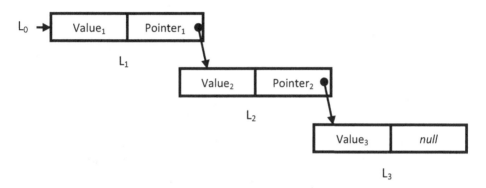

Figure 1-1. *One-dimensional linked list*

In Figure 1-1, L_0 is the first element (or *head* or *header* of the list) and is the access point to the list; it's a pointer that links the first element with the data of the linked list. If $\text{next}[L_0]$ = NIL, the list is empty.

The order in a linked list is determined by a pointer in each element. To access a node of a linked list, we start with the first node of the list and traverse the pointer chain until the node is reached. Unlike arrays, linked lists do not require preliminary reservation of the computer memory. It is possible to insert or delete an element in the list by reconnecting pointers, but we need to scroll the list and reach the appropriate node, because the reference to an element is present only in the previous one.

If we wanted to insert a new node (L_{new}) between two existing nodes (L_1 and L_2), we would first link the new pointer (Pointer_{new}) to the next node (L_2) and then link the pointer to the previous element (Pointer_1) to the new node (L_{new}), as shown in Figure 1-2. Otherwise, we would lose the link to the next element.

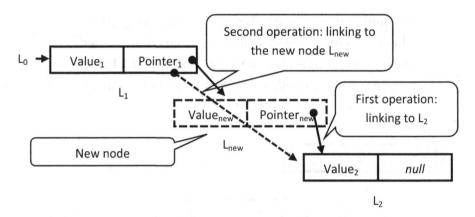

Figure 1-2. *Insertion in one-dimensional linked list*

If we wanted to delete a node (L_2) between two existing nodes (L_1 and L_3), we would first link the new pointer (Pointer$_1$) to the next node (L_3) and then delete the element (L_2), as depicted in Figure 1-3. Otherwise, we would lose the link to the next element.

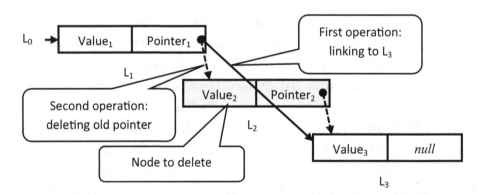

Figure 1-3. *Deletion in one-dimensional linked list*

Furthermore, it is possible to define a doubly linked list (different from a singly linked list that has one pointer) that is a data structure with a field for the data and two fields for two pointers: next pointer (which points to its successor) and prev pointer (which points to its predecessor). This structure is more complex because it must handle two pointers and obviously uses more memory, but it assures better performance and simplicity in searching and managing elements in the list.

Stack

A *stack* is a dynamic data structure in which insertions and deletions can be done only at the top of the stack (usually in a vertical visualization of the stack, like a stack of plates). In fact, the stack implements a *last-in, first-out* (LIFO) policy. Specifically, inserted elements (push operations) are added at the top of the stack, and deleted elements (pop operations) are removed from the top of the stack (the most recently inserted), as illustrated in Figure 1-4. The stack is indispensable for implementing recursive algorithms.

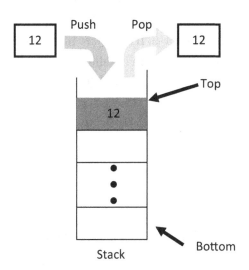

Figure 1-4. *Stack*

Queue

A *queue* is a dynamic data structure in which insertions (the input is an operation of enqueue) can be done from one end and deletions (the output is an operation of dequeue) can be done from the other end. The element deleted is the one stored for the longest time. This is called a *first-in, first-out* (FIFO) policy. Figure 1-5 shows an example.

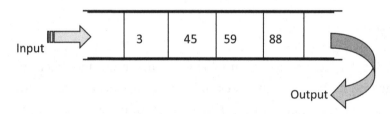

Figure 1-5. *Queue*

Graph

A *graph* is a data structure characterized by a collection of points in the plane called *nodes* (or *vertices*), some of them connected by line segments called *arcs*, as shown in Figure 1-6. If every arc has a direction, indicated with an arrow on one edge, the graph is called *directed*. In a directed graph, it is possible to traverse the graph only by following the direction of the arrow from a node to another.

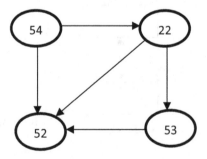

Figure 1-6. *Graph*

Tree

A *tree* is a data structure characterized by a connected acyclic graph. In other words, there is no node connected to a previous one through an arc that can eventually create a loop in the data structure. The tree has a root (at the top) and a set of child nodes, connected by arcs. The number of arcs in a tree is always one less than the number of its nodes. In particular, a binary tree has no more than two children for every node, as depicted in Figure 1-7.

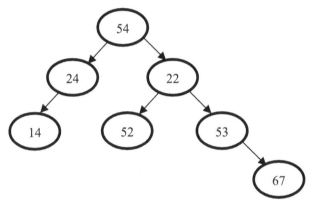

Figure 1-7. *Tree*

Hash Table

A *hash table* is a data structure characterized by a sequence of *n* couples of items: `<key,value>`. It is useful for implementing dynamic sets or dictionaries (for example, a symbol table for a compiler in a computer language). It is a direct-access table, which supports the operations of insertion, deletion, and searching. In this data structure, the key is calculated according to the value to be stored, as an interesting alternative to the use of arrays, especially in the searching algorithms. In fact, hash tables perform extremely well when searched and become an effective alternative to directly addressing an array, because the index is computed from the key with particular hashing algorithms, instead of using the key as an array index directly. It is also possible to handle *collisions* in which more than one key maps to the same index.

11

Record

A *record* (or *struct*) is a collection of a fixed number of elements (the fields of the record). Each field can be a different data type. For example, if we wanted to store an address, we would write a record containing some string fields (i.e., name, surname, city, etc.) and some numeric fields (i.e., ZIP code or postal code). For example, we would write the following:

- Name

- Surname

- Postal code

- City

- Nation

Figure 1-8 shows an example.

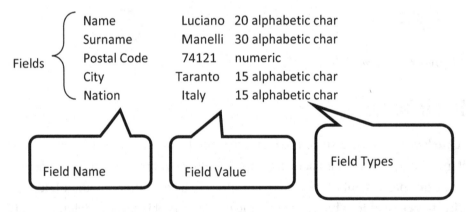

Figure 1-8. *Record*

File

A *file* is a set of data entities stored on a computer disk and consisting of primitive or structured data that can be written, read, deleted, and updated.

12

CHAPTER 2

Design of Algorithms

An *algorithm* is a well-defined computational procedure for solving a problem with an understandable language, intended for eventual computer implementation. The algorithm takes some values as *input* and produces, after some computations, some values as *output*. Specifically, the algorithm presents a finite series of instructions that are translated into a programming language and processed by a computer or another electronic device.

Informally, algorithms are used in our daily lives. For example, it is possible to describe a series of operations such as the instructions in a recipe, the instructions for a washing machine, or the instructions for a cell phone. Think of your favorite food: we start with the ingredients (input data), prepare the specific dish described in the recipe (set of instructions), and, finally, present the prepared dish (output data). Algorithm analysis is an important part of any programming language for solving a computational problem. There are many programming languages, but it will always be easy to program if you have an understanding of how to use algorithms to solve problems.

© Luciano Manelli 2020
L. Manelli, *Introducing Algorithms in C*, https://doi.org/10.1007/978-1-4842-5623-7_2

Algorithm Basics

These are the fundamental facts about an algorithm:

- An algorithm is a sequence of unambiguous instructions understood by everyone in the same way.

- An algorithm requires instructions that can be executed by someone capable of understanding and following the instructions given.

- An algorithm requires a finite set of instructions (with a start and an end).

- An algorithm requires a finite set of input/output values.

- An algorithm requires the output to be produced in a finite amount of time.

- An algorithm is required to be valid, if possible, for a class of problems, i.e. for a set of similar problems (generality of the problems the algorithm solves: the goal is to create an algorithm that let us to prepare a set of recipes and not create a different algorithm for each recipe).

An algorithm has to possess other important qualities, such as efficiency (how fast the algorithm runs and how much memory it uses) and simplicity (easy to understand and easy to program). Furthermore, it is possible that the same algorithm can be represented in different ways and that several algorithms may exist for solving the same computational problem.

If we want to develop a good algorithm, we have to analyze a problem. To do this effectively, we can divide a problem into subproblems (the *divide and conquer* technique), manipulating the relationships and the solutions into smaller problems to solve a given instance of a problem. This is a *top-down* approach. A *bottom-up* approach, by contrast, operates in an inductive way. It begins with separate elements (subproblems) and merges them into successively larger solutions to solve one bigger problem. While this approach can lead to an algorithm that solves common subproblems, the solutions to some of these subproblems are often not necessary for getting a solution to the bigger problem. It is natural to combine the strengths of the top-down and bottom-up approaches to solve a problem in the best way. The first approach gives us an overall view of the problem necessary for a good design and allows a better organization for working in teams; the second approach helps us with the reusability of the software and of the existing code.

At this point, it is important to emphasize the *design* of algorithms. Good design is achieved through a good description of the problem and its solution. Tables can help us understand the evolution of the algorithm and to validate it, and graphical tools can help us communicate the solution to the stakeholders.

Therefore, we first will study a flow chart, which is an important "tool" for specifying algorithms. It is a method of expressing and designing an algorithm with a collection of connected geometric shapes containing inputs, computations, choices, and descriptions of the algorithm's steps. We will analyze and study some of the most important classes of algorithms to solve problems of searching and sorting with flow charts.

Flow charts work best for simple algorithms, but this technique represents the starting point for other formal or informal graphic specification languages. Furthermore, flow charts provide us with a graphical tool for designing algorithms for new problems.

The second step is to convert the flow chart into a computer program written in a particular language, which is C in this book (see the next chapter).

Eventually, *pseudocode* (a mixture of a natural language and a programming language that is human-readable) can help you if you do not want to depend on a particular programming language (and if you want to avoid overly complex flow charts).

Now, we will focus on some important algorithms from different areas of computing that are used to solve problems according to a design idea. These are general problem-solving strategies, applicable to new and unknown problems. By the end of this chapter, we should be able to design and analyze new algorithms to solve new problems.

This book does not contain a recipe for designing an algorithm for arbitrary problems; instead, it provides techniques for analyzing a problem and studying an algorithm with flow charts and description tables to solve the problem. The chapter discusses several important issues related to the design of algorithms and their application. The aim is to provide techniques to solve the most common problems in real-life applications.

Remember that if an algorithm is easy to understand and to analyze, the resulting program usually contains fewer bugs!

Flow Chart and Structured Programming

As mentioned, we will use a graphical tool for the analysis and development of an algorithm: the flow chart. This type of diagram, which can represent an algorithm or a workflow or a process, describes the steps of an algorithm with boxes of various kinds (rectangles, parallelograms, ovals, and diamonds) connected by arrows. Graphical tools are widely used in business to visually explain computer, procedural, or statistical ideas and notions; Unified Modeling Language (UML) and Business Process Model and Notation (BPMN) are two examples of standards used.

The flow chart is the graphical basis of structured programming, which is a programming paradigm based on the use of block structures, loops, and three fundamental control structures (sequence, selection, and iteration). This paradigm celebrates quality and clarity in contrast to the use of chaotic jumps.

Flow charts are composed of building blocks, which differ according to their shapes and to the functions they perform in algorithms. The blocks are joined by oriented arcs, which express the direction of the algorithmic flow (usually from top to bottom). The following are the most important shapes:

- **Terminal block**: This is represented as a circle (or an oval) placed at the beginning (or at the end) of an algorithm; it is unique for any given algorithm, and it shows the point at which the execution begins (or ends).

- **Process block**: This is represented as a rectangle, and it indicates the execution of an operation within the algorithm.

- **Decision block (or test)**: This is represented as a diamond, and it is used to select two different paths depending on the result of the condition (yes/no or true/false) written within the block.

- **Input/output block**: This is represented as a parallelogram, and it is used as either an input operation (acquisition of a value from the keyboard, an image from a scanner, a measure from a sensor, a file from the hard disk, a result of a query on the database, etc.) or an output operation (the display of a value on the screen of a computer or other output devices such as a printer, writing a value to the database, or sending a command to an actuator).

- **Line**: This is represented as an arrow starting from one shape and ending at another shape.

The shapes are shown in Figure 2-1.

Terminal	Process	Decision	Input/Output	Line
Block	Block	Block	Block	

Figure 2-1. *Flow chart blocks*

Different blocks are linked to each other with lines. Two lines never cross to avoid ambiguity; it can be useful to insert an arc on a line to avoid crossing them. Different blocks are combined with each other to achieve an algorithmic solution to a problem.

Structured programming defines the rules for composing and combining the various blocks and allows the creation of the algorithmic flows with standard instructions. The following are the control constructs of this paradigm:

- **Sequence**: This is the most used construct; it defines a series of statements or subroutines that have to be executed in sequence. For example, the instructions for a phone call would have three blocks (Unlock Phone, Type in Phone Number, and Make Call). Figure 2-2 illustrates this control construct with a simple example.

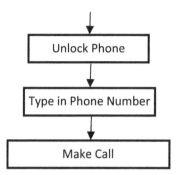

Figure 2-2. *Sequence example*

- **Selection**: This construct allows you to choose two different paths depending on a choice. For example, it is an answer to the question "Is the condition verified?" and can be true or false. The standard selection has two outputs.

  This condition is usually expressed with the keywords if/else or if/then/else and endif. The following is an example with pseudocode:

  if< question/test is true>
  "execute" <instructions **1**>
   else< question/test is false>
   "execute" < instructions **2**>

The keyword execute depends on the programming language. Figure 2-3 shows an example of the selection construct.

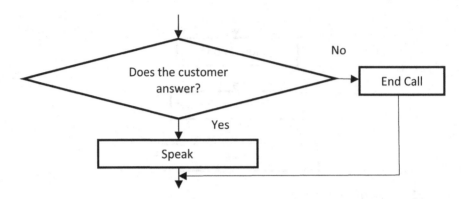

Figure 2-3. *Selection example*

- **Iteration**: This construct is used when a set of instructions has to be executed several times until the occurrence of a condition (which can be true or false), i.e., until the program reaches a particular state. This is usually expressed with keywords such as while or repeat, for, or do/until.

repeat and while

The two main types of iteration are repeat and while. The difference is in how we test the conditions. The while checks whether the condition is verified at the beginning of the iteration; the repeat checks the same condition at the end of the cycle. The while loop is better, especially if we are not sure that the condition will occur. Figure 2-4 and Figure 2-5 illustrate these types of iteration.

For example, if we are searching for a keyword on the Internet (for example, on Google), the search engine exposes results (with a while loop) as a list with a preview. If our search does not produce any results, the while loop is not executed, and the lines of code (to display the results) are not executed and visible.

Here's an example of the while loop, with pseudocode:

```
while < question/test is true>
  "execute" < instructions >
```

Note that the keyword execute depends on the programming language.

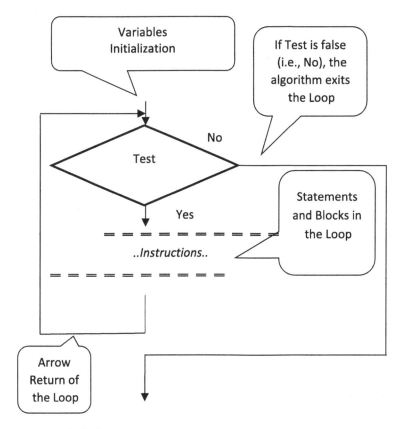

Figure 2-4. *while loop*

The following is an example of the repeat loop in pseudocode:

repeat (execute) < instructions > "until" < question/test is true >

Note that the keywords repeat and until depend on the programming language.

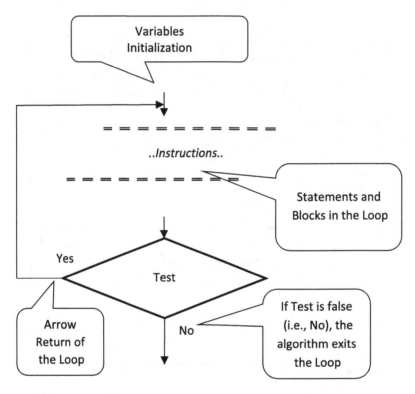

Figure 2-5. *repeat loop*

We can combine the structures and get a loop. In Figure 2-6, after closing the call, it continues until the customer answers.

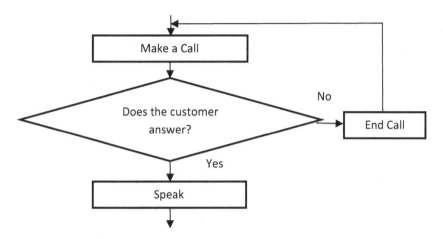

Figure 2-6. *Loop example*

for

If the number of iterations is determined *a priori*, it is possible to use the for construct. The for statement allows the use of a single-line command in which the number of iterations to perform are counted. It is used to manage arrays (the length is usually known *a priori*). It is possible to define the following pseudocode:

for< iteration index> "from" <lower index> "to" <top index> "using" <step> *execute* < instructions >

Note that the keywords from, to, and using depend on the programming language, and the encoding depends on the programming language.

In the following sections, we will use the while and for loops.

The Algorithms

It is necessary to develop a paradigm to understand a computational problem. This paradigm can be similar to what we did earlier, or it can be a totally new approach. It is also important to understand the existing algorithms used to achieve the best results for any computational problem. That is why, in this section, we will study some algorithms before introducing any programming.

In this way, we can focus on problem-solving by creating sets of specifications/instructions for a specific domain (i.e., "how to do it"), rather than on the details of writing low-level programming instructions (i.e., "what to do"), which is discussed in the next chapter.

Without further ado, we will now build the significant algorithms that support the practice problems and analyze the instructions one step at a time.

Sum of Three Numbers

Figure 2-7 shows the flow chart of the "sum of three numbers" algorithm that adds three integers read from input (e.g., from the keyboard). This algorithm is simple because it reads the three numbers in sequence, stores the numbers in three variables (a, b, c), and adds the variables and prints the sum.

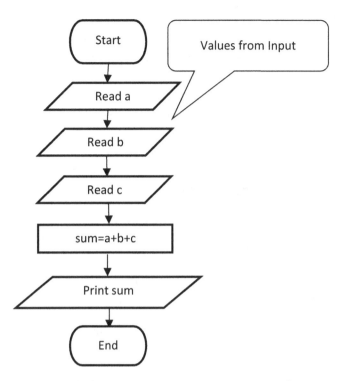

Figure 2-7. *Flow chart of the "sum of three numbers" algorithm*

Sum of *n* Numbers in a Loop

Figure 2-8 shows the flow chart of the "sum of *n* numbers in a loop" algorithm that adds *n* integers read from input (e.g., from the keyboard) with the help of a loop. The algorithm asks for *n* number of elements to be added, and then it reads the numbers in a cycle. At each iteration, these numbers are added to the sum (initialized equal to 0). Finally, it prints the sum.

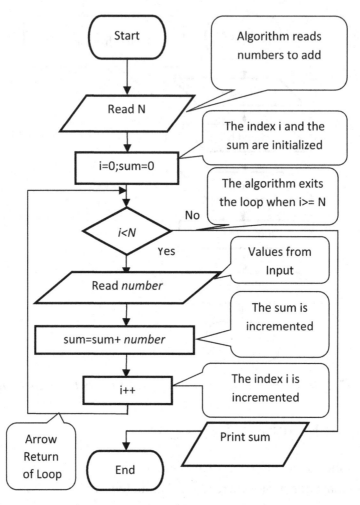

Figure 2-8. *Flow chart of the "sum of n numbers in a loop" algorithm*

Table 2-1 shows the process of summing three elements from the input (in order: 25, 10, 15) in an array of length 3 (N=3).

Table 2-1. *Adding Input Numbers in Loop Values*

Iteration	i	Input Number	Sum	i++
1°	0	25	25	1
2°	1	15	40	2
3°	2	30	70	3

Storing Numbers Within an Array

This example assigns values to an array. An array is used to store multiple values in a single variable (for example, a list of names). We will access the values by referring to an index number.

In the flow chart in Figure 2-9, we will store a set of integer numbers read from an input (for example, input from a keyboard). The length of the array is N, which is also read by input. The algorithm implements a while loop with index i. On each iteration, the input value is read and stored (v[i]=number) in the corresponding element of the array of position i. This happens until the condition (the end of the array) becomes false.

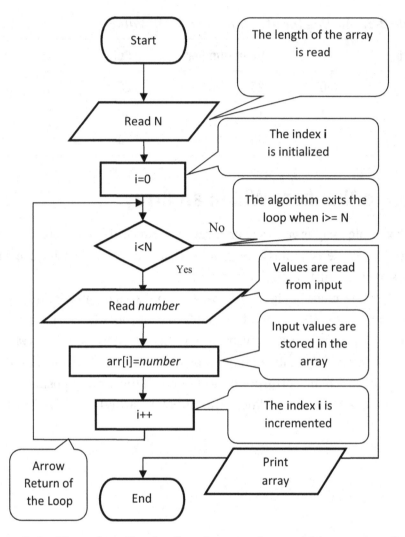

Figure 2-9. *Flow chart for the "storing numbers within an array"*
algorithm

Table 2-2 shows the loading of five elements from input (in order: 2, 3, 4, 5, 28) in an array of length 5 (N=5). The iteration step corresponds to a new iteration of the algorithm starting from the condition of verification (i < N). A value of 0 is assigned to index i. On each iteration, the index i is incremented until i >= N, when the algorithm exits the loop, because each element of the array has been analyzed.

Table 2-2. *Storing Input Variables Within an Array: Values*

Iteration	i	Value	arr[i]	i++
1°	0	2	2	1
2°	1	3	3	2
3°	2	4	4	3
4°	3	5	5	4
5°	4	28	28	5
6°	5	-	-	-

As shown in the table, the variable values at each step of the iteration are as follows:

- The iteration step
- The index value i
- The value read in input
- The value stored in the array v[i]
- The incremented value of index i at the end of cycle

The increase is indicated with i++ (similar to how it's done the programming languages C and Java), and it is equivalent to i = i + 1. In other words, the value of the index i is replaced with the value of the same index i incremented by 1.

Array Exercise

As an example, we will design the flow chart of an algorithm that reads 10 integers, calculates 50 percent of each input value (we will multiply by 0.5: v[i]=v[i]*0.5), and finally executes the sum of the modified values. For the readability and modularity of the algorithm, it is always recommended to separate the processing step from the stored input so that it is possible to focus only on the operations on the data.

Therefore, we will consider the array already filled (see the previous section).

We will define the sum variable to store and increase the value of the sum. At each cycle, an element of the array (identified by the index i – v[i]) is modified and subsequently added to the previous value of the sum (sum=sum+ v[i]).

At the end, we will print the sum, as shown in Figure 2-10.

In this case, the sum variable is initialized to 0.

If it had been requested, the product variable would have been initialized to 1.

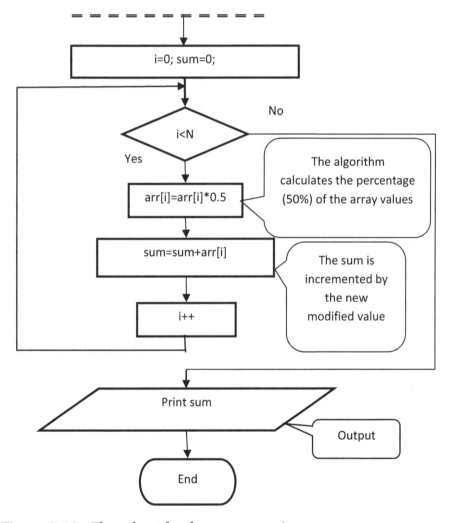

Figure 2-10. *Flow chart for the array exercise*

Table 2-3 shows the results of the array exercise, assuming that an array of eight elements (of length N=8) is loaded (in order: 20, 12, 16, 50, 4, 6, 10, 8).

Table 2-3. *Array Exercise: Values*

Iteration	i	v[i]	arr[i]*50%	sum
1°	0	20	10	10
2°	1	12	6	16
3°	2	16	8	24
4°	3	50	25	49
5°	4	4	2	51
6°	5	6	3	54
7°	6	10	5	59
8°	7	8	4	63
9°	8	-	-	-

Converting a Decimal Number to a Binary Number

An easy method of converting an integer to a binary number is to write down the integer and divide it by 2 so that the remainder of each operation is a 1 or a 0. (When the dividend is even, the binary remainder is 0, and when the dividend is odd, the binary remainder is 1.) It is necessary to continue dividing the new quotient by 2 until the quotient equals 0. Therefore, it is possible to build the binary number as a sequence of digits (0 or 1). At the end, we can write out the result starting with the bottom remainder and reading the sequence of remainders upward to the top.

The algorithm has to do the following steps:

1. Control the integer input value.

2. Divide by 2 until the quotient is 0.

3. Write out the result, reading the remainder from the last to the first.

How can we translate this into a flow chart? How can we design the algorithm? These are the steps:

1. We will suppose 8 bits, so the input decimal number N must be 0<= N <= 255;.

2. We will use an array to set the binary digit.

3. Moreover, for an 8-bit binary number, the algorithm has to insert digits in an array (which has 0 preassigned values for each element).

4. We will divide the number by 2 and insert the remainder in the array (the first remainder will be set in the v[0] element, the second remainder will be set in the v[1] element, and the others will be in the next elements in turn).

5. We will divide the new quotient by 2 until it is 0.

6. At the end of the algorithm, we will write out the result, reading the array from the last element (v[7], the most significant bit) to the first (v[0], the least significant bit) to reverse the order of the array as built in the previous step. This will represent the number in the correct way.

In a programming language, there are usually two functions that allow you to obtain the two values.

• The DIV function: Obtains the remainder

• The MOD function: Obtains the quotient

Here's an example that converts the integer 12 to a binary number:

$12:2=6$ *(quotient) ; remainder =0 ➜ in v[0]*

$6:2=3$ *(quotient) ; remainder =0 ➜ in v[1]*

$3:2=1$ *(quotient) ; remainder =1 ➜ in v[2]*

$1:2=0$ *(quotient) ; remainder =1 ➜ in v[3]*

Final quotient = 0 ➜ STOP

Therefore:

12_{10} ➜ 1100_2

In this case, the initialized array is 0000 0000.
The array at the end of the loop is 0011 0000.
Now, the array read in reverse is 0000 1100.
Here's an example that converts the integer 17 to a binary number.

$17:2=8$ *(quotient) ; remainder = 1 ➜ in v[0]*

$8:2=4$ *(quotient) ; remainder = 0 ➜ in v[1]*

$4:2=2$ *(quotient) ; remainder = 0 ➜ in v[2]*

$2:2=1$ *(quotient) ; remainder = 0 ➜ in v[3]*

$1:2=0$ *(quotient) ; remainder = 1 ➜ in v[4]*

Final quotient = 0 ➜ STOP

Therefore:

17_{10} ➜ 10001_2

The initialized array is 0000 0000.
The array at the end of the loop is 10001 000.
The final array 000 10001
Figure 2-11 shows the design of the algorithm.

We can check the input number with a control point because, with 8 bits, it is possible to represent a positive number between 0 and 255, and we want to accept only those values.

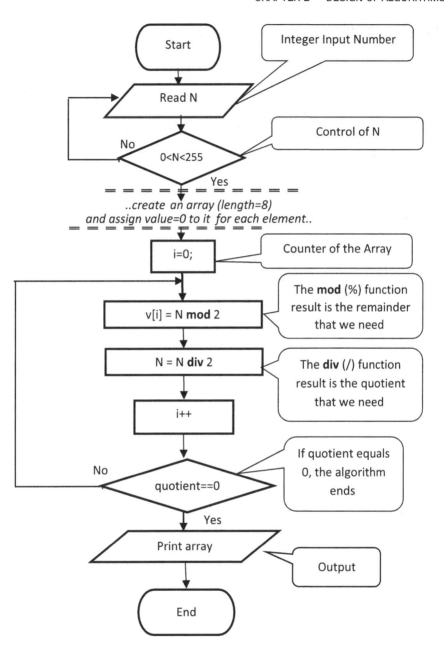

Figure 2-11. *Flow chart for "converting a decimal number to a binary number" algorithm*

Maximum/Minimum Search

Now we will study the algorithm shown in Figure 2-12 that reads *n* numbers and computes the maximum value and the minimum value. After loading an array of length N, the algorithm initializes the variables like so: i = 1 (we start from the second element of the array, because the first element is set to minimum or maximum), then min = v [0], and finally max = v [0].

The first condition, for searching for the minimum, is v [i] < min. If the element under investigation is smaller than the current minimum, it is set equal to the min.

The second condition, for searching for the maximum, is v [i] > max. If the item under investigation is greater than the current maximum, it is set equal to max.

Finally, the algorithm increases the index i: i ++. At the end of the array, the condition (i<N) is no longer satisfied, and the algorithm exits the loop.

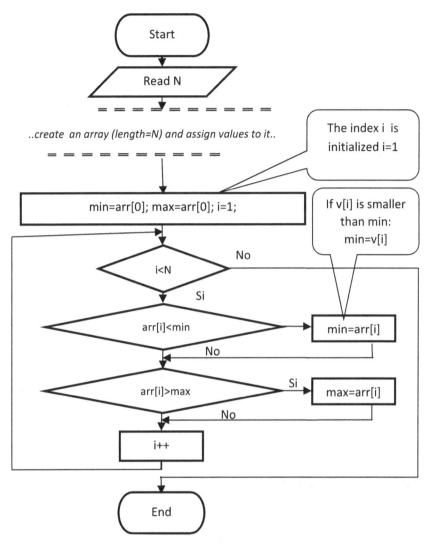

Figure 2-12. *Flow chart for the "maximum/minimum search" algorithm*

Table 2-4 shows the results of the exercise, assuming that an array of eight elements (of length N=8) is loaded (in order: 20, 12, 16, 50, 4, 6, 10, 8). The initial conditions set the maximum and the minimum equal to the first element of the array. In this way, the first comparison is made with a valid value, and the first step of the iteration sets the index equal to 1.

Table 2-4. *Maximum/Minimum Search: Values*

Iteration	i	arr[i]	min	max
0°	0	20	20	20
1°	1	12	12	20
2°	2	16	12	20
3°	3	50	12	50
4°	4	4	4	50
5°	5	6	4	50
6°	6	10	4	50
7°	7	8	4	50
8°	8	-	-	-

Searching Problem

The searching problem deals with finding a value (the search key) in a given set of elements of the same type. There are a lot of searching algorithms; we will analyze two: sequential search and binary search. An efficient searching algorithm has implications for real-world applications, and it is a challenge to choose one that fits all situations best.

Linear/Sequential Search

In this section, we will study the algorithm that searches a number in an array of unsorted numbers. We will use a Boolean variable called found, which is set equal to true when the algorithm finds the number we are searching for (if it exists in the elements stored in the array). On each iteration, the algorithm compares the numbers in the array with the search key. Furthermore, on each iteration, the loop condition controls whether the number has been found. In this way, if the number was found, the Boolean variable found is set to true, and we can exit the loop, avoiding further unnecessary iterations. After preloading an array of length N and reading the search key in the input, the algorithm compares all the elements of the array in a loop, looking for the search key. The loop continues until the search key is found (a successful search) or the end of the array is found (a failure). In both cases, the algorithm exits the loop. Figure 2-13 illustrates the flow chart. This typology of search is simple, but it has bad efficiency.

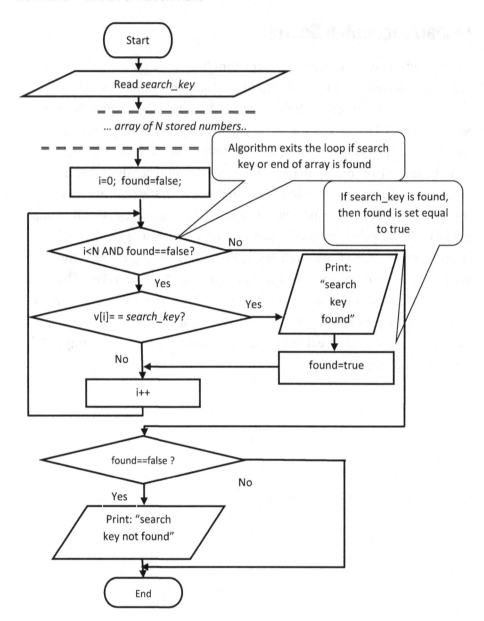

Figure 2-13. *Flow chart of the "linear/sequential search" algorithm*

The iterations and the results of the algorithm are given in Table 2-5, assuming that an array of five elements (of length N=5) is loaded (in order: 28, 14, 61, 49, 3) and that we are looking for a search key of 49. The initial condition sets the variable found equal to false. The algorithm avoids the comparison with the last element of the array because the search key is found in the fourth iteration.

Table 2-5. *Linear/Sequential Search: Values*

Iteration	i	i < N	arr[i]	arr[i] = search key	found = false
1°	0	Yes	28	NO	Yes
2°	1	Yes	14	NO	Yes
3°	2	Yes	61	NO	Yes
4°	3	Yes	49	Yes (found = true)	NO
5°	4	Yes	-	-	-

At the end of the algorithm, if the condition found is equal to false, the displayed message will be "search key not found." Otherwise, the displayed message will be "search key found."

Binary Search

In this section, we will study the algorithm that searches for a number in an array of sorted integers. In this case (a sorted array), it is possible to apply an algorithm that reduces the number of iterations and consequently increases the speed and efficiency of the algorithm. After preloading an array of length N and reading the search key in the input, the algorithm compares the middle element of the array with the other elements and proceeds to search the higher or lower sublist in a recursive way. The binary search is widely used since it is fast. It is sufficient to evaluate whether the searched number is in the middle of the array. If this condition is not satisfied, the searched number can be higher or lower than the number in the middle.

If the number to look for is greater than the number in the middle, then we have to search for it in the lower half of the array; if it's less than the middle one, then we search for it in the higher half, as explained in Figure 2-14.

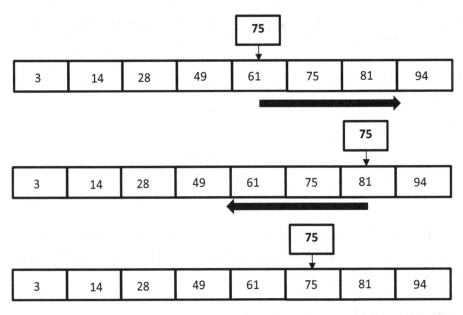

Figure 2-14. *How binary search works*

The algorithm stops when a match is encountered, and it returns the middle index (a successful search); if it continues until there are no values left, then it generates a state of inconsistency (a failure).

The name of this type of research comes from each iteration reducing the size of the array by one-half to analyze while searching the key. The search key can be to the right or left (or above or below), based on a central element of comparison. Each iteration divides by 2 the array of length *n*

($n/2$, $n/4$, and so on), so the maximum number of comparisons/iterations is equal to $\log_2 n$.

After loading an array sorted in nondecreasing order of length N and reading the *search key*, the initial conditions are set: lft (*left*) = 0, rig (*right*) = N-1, pos (*position of the key*) = -1. The next condition is sn <= dx AND pos = -1, which requires continuing the iterations if both conditions are met. The algorithm calculates the middle with mdl = (lft + rig + 1) / 2 and checks the condition of equality between the search key and the element in position mdl. If the condition is not satisfied (the element is not found), it is evaluated whether the number to look for is larger or smaller than the selected one of the array. Depending on the answer, the algorithm sets lft = mdl + 1, and the search continues on the lower half of the array, or it sets rig = mdl-1, and the search continues on the upper half of the array. The search continues until the key is found and its position is returned or there are no more elements left to search for in the array, generating a state of inconsistency: rig<lft (the initial condition sn <= dx is no longer verified and therefore the number was not found)!

Figure 2-15 illustrates the flow chart.

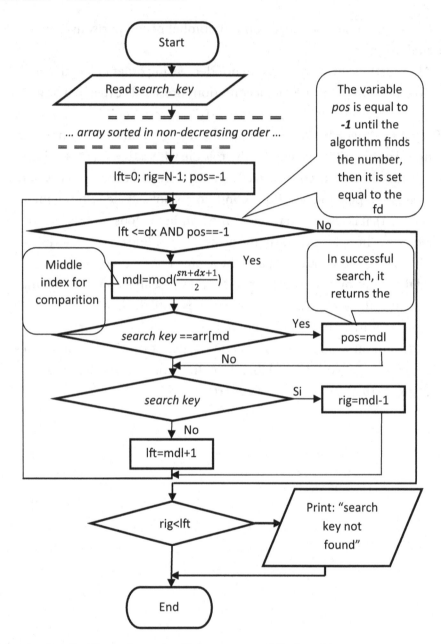

Figure 2-15. *Flow chart for "binary search" algorithm*

The iterations and the results of the algorithm are given in Table 2-6, assuming that an array sorted in nondecreasing order of eight elements (of length N=8) is loaded (in order: 3, 14, 28, 49, 61, 75, 81, 94) and that we are looking for a search key of 75. The algorithm compares the search key to 61 (mdl). The search key is larger, so we will repeat the process with the sublist: 75, 81, 94. Then, the algorithm compares the search key to 81 (new mdl). The search key is smaller, so we will repeat the process with the sublist of 75. Then, the algorithm compares the search key to 75 (new mdl). The search key equals 75, so the position is returned! The search item was found in three steps.

Table 2-6. *Binary Search: Values for Successful Search*

Iteration	lft	rig	pos	lft<=rig AND pos=-1	mdl	arr[mdl]	search_ key = arr[mdl]	search_key < arr[mdl]	lft<=rig
1°	0	7	-1	YES	4	61	NO	NO (lft=mdl+1)	YES
2°	5	7	-1	YES	6	81	NO	YES (rig=mdl-1)	YES
3°	5	5	-1	YES	5	75	YES		YES
4°	5	5	5	NO (pos=5)	-	-	-	-	YES

Suppose now we are looking for the number 50, as shown in Table 2-7.

Table 2-7. *Binary Search: Values for Failure*

Iteration	lft	rig	pos	lft<=rig AND pos=-1	mdl	arr[mdl]	search_ key = arr[mdl]	search_key <arr[mdl]	lft<=rig
1°	0	7	-1	YES	4	61	NO	YES (rig=mdl-1)	YES
2°	0	5	-1	YES	3	49	NO	NO (lft=mdl+1)	YES
3°	4	5	-1	YES	5	75	NO	YES (rig=mdl-1)	YES
4°	4	4	-1	YES	4	61	NO	YES (rig=mdl-1)	YES
5°	4	3	-1	NO (dx>sx)	-	-	-	-	NO

In this case, the value is not found.

Sorting Problem

The sorting problem deals with rearranging the elements of an array in a nondecreasing order. Therefore, we can sort lists of numbers, characters from an alphabet, and records. A sorted list is important because we can use an efficient searching algorithm to look for an element (for example, in an Internet search, in a database search, in dictionaries, or in telephone books). This has implications for real-world applications, but it is a challenge to choose one that fits all situations best. There are good sorting algorithms that sort an array, but no algorithm is the best solution in all situations. Some are simple but slow, while others are faster but complex. We will study two important algorithms.

Bubble Sort

Now we will study the "bubble sort" algorithm shown in Figure 2-16 that sorts an array of integers in a nondecreasing order. This algorithm compares each pair of adjacent elements of the array and exchanges them if they are out of order in a recursive way; therefore, we will see a "bubbling up" of the largest element to the last position on the array as a bubble. After loading an array of length N, the algorithm initializes the variable i equal to 0 (condition for external loop i <N) in the external loop, as well as the variable j equal to N-1 (condition for internal loop j>i) in the internal loop. If the test block arr[j] <arr[j-1] is true, there is an exchange between the elements arr[j] and arr[j-1] (this is the *swapping* operation into a separate function, swap). At the end, the sorted array is printed.

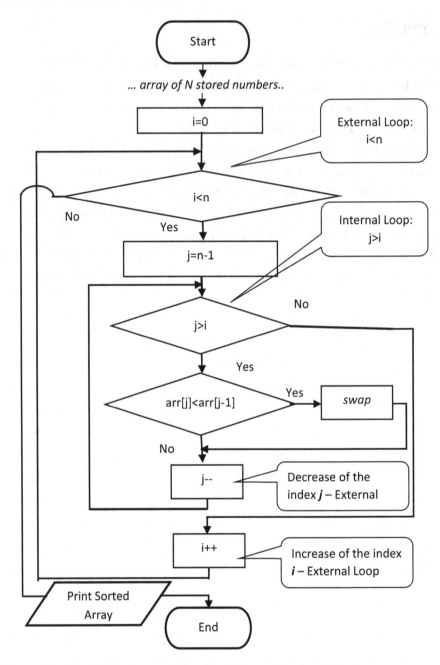

Figure 2-16. *Flow chart of the "bubble sort" algorithm*

It is important to analyze the swap function. The way to swap two variables is to use a third temporary variable (temp), as shown in Table 2-8 (exchanging between the variables, or elements of the array, arr[2] and arr[3]).

Table 2-8. *Swapping Steps*

Steps	arr[2]	arr[3]	temp
arr[2]=x; arr[3]=y	x	y	-
1) temp = V[2]	x	y	x
2) arr[2] = arr[3]	y	y	x
3) arr[3] = temp	y	x	x

Table 2-9 shows an example with two variables, a=5 and b=6. Swapping the two values means assigning the value of a to the variable b and to assign the value of b to the variable a. If we assign the value of b to the variable a (a = b (= 6)), we lose the contents of a since they are overwritten. So, we will simply assign the value of a to a temp variable: temp = a (= 5). Then, we assign the value of b to the variable a. Finally, we will assign the value of the temp variable to b = temp (= 5).

Table 2-9. *Swap Steps: An Example*

Steps	a	b	temp
a=5; b=6	5	6	-
1) temp = a	5	6	5
2) a = b	6	6	5
3) b = temp	6	5	5

The iterations and the results of the algorithm are given in Table 2-10, assuming that an array of five elements is loaded (in order: 28, 14, 61, 49, 3).

Table 2-10. *Bubble Sort: Table of Values*

Iteration	i	i<n	j	j>i	arr[j]	arr[j-1]	arr[j]<arr[j-1]	SWAP (arr[j] and arr[j-1])
1°	0	YES	4	YES	3	49	YES (swap)	{28, 14, 61, *3*, 49}
2°	0	YES	3	YES	3	61	YES (swap)	{28, 14, *3*, 61, 49}
3°	0	YES	2	YES	3	14	YES (swap)	{28, *3*, 14, 61, 49}
4°	0	YES	1	YES	3	28	YES (swap)	{*3*, 28, 14, 61, 49}
5°	0	YES	0	NO	-			
6°	1	YES	4	YES	49	61	YES (swap)	{3, 28, 14, *49*, 61}
7°	1	YES	3	YES	49	14	NO (no swap)	
8°	1	YES	2	YES	14	28	SI (swap)	{3, *14*, 28, 49, 61}
9°	1	YES	1	NO	-			
10°	2	YES	4	YES	61	49	NO (no swap)	
11°	2	YES	3	YES	49	28	NO (no swap)	
12°	2	YES	2	NO	-			
13°	3	YES	4	YES	61	49	NO (no swap)	
14°	3	YES	3	NO	-			
15°	4	YES	4	NO	-			
16°	5	NO	-					

Selection Sort

In this section, we will study the "selection sort" algorithm shown in Figure 2-17 that sorts an array of integers in a nondecreasing order. This algorithm scans the n elements stored in an array (arr) to find its smallest element and exchanges it with the first element (arr[0]). Then, the algorithm scans the last n-1 elements of the array to find the second smallest element of A and exchanges it with the second element (arr[1]) of the array. The algorithm continues in this manner for the n-1 elements of the array (the last element is consequently sorted). In this case, the basic operation is a key comparison: A[j]<A[min].

This algorithm is different from the previous algorithm because the exchange is carried out only once at the end of the cycle by selecting the right index.

After loading an array of length N, the algorithm initializes the variable i equal to 0 (the condition for the external loop i < N-1) in the external loop, and the variable j is equal to i+1 and imin=i (the condition for the internal loop j<N) in the internal loop. If the test block arr[j] <arr[imin] is true, imin is set equal to i. At the end of the internal loop, there is an exchange between the elements arr[j] and arr[imin]. At the end, the sorted array is printed. In this case, the number of swaps depends only on the array size.

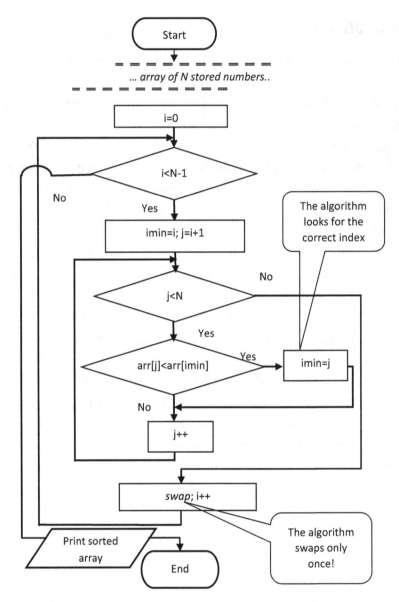

Figure 2-17. *Flow chart of the "selection sort" algorithm*

The iterations and the results of the algorithm are given in Table 2-11, assuming that an array of five elements is loaded (in order: 28, 14, 61, 49, 3).

Table 2-11. *Selection Sort: Values*

Itaration	i	i<n-1	imin	j	j<n	arr[j]	arr[imin]	arr[j] < arr[imin]	imin=i	SWAP (arr[i] and arr[imin])
1°	0	YES	0	1	YES	14	28	YES (imin=j)		
2°	0	YES	1	2	YES	61	14	NO		
3°	0	YES	1	3	YES	49	14	NO		
4°	0	YES	1	4	YES	3	14	YES (imin=j)		
5°	0	YES	4	5	NO: it exits internal loop				NO (swap)	{3, 14, 61, 49, 28}
6°	1	YES	1	2	YES	61	14	NO		
7°	1	YES	1	3	YES	49	14	NO		
8°	1	YES	1	4	YES	28	14	NO		
9°	1	YES	1	5	NO				YES (no swap)	
10°	2	YES	2	3	YES	49	61	SI (imin=j)		

(*continued*)

Table 2-11. (*continued*)

Itaration	i	i<n-1	imin	j	j<n	arr[j]	arr[imin]	arr[j] < arr[imin]	imin=i	SWAP (arr[i] and arr[imin])
11°	2	YES	3	4	YES	28	49	SI (imin=j)		
12°	2	YES	4	5	NO				NO (swap)	{3, 14, 28, 49, 61}
13°	3	YES	3	4	YES	61	49	NO		
14°	3	YES	3	5	NO				YES (no swap)	
15°	4	NO	-	-	-	-	-	-	-	-

Merging of Two Sorted Arrays

In this section, we will study the "merging of two sorted arrays" algorithm shown in Figure 2-18 that merges two sorted arrays (v of length N, and w of length M). This algorithm scans the elements of the two arrays and compares them. The smaller of them is added to a new array being constructed (z of length N+M). After that, only the index of the array of the smaller element is incremented. We will repeat this operation until one of the two given arrays is exhausted.

The remaining elements of the other array are stored in the end of the new array.

In the flow chart shown in Figure 2-18, notice that the blocks in the gray shape are not formally structured. We've done this because it is simpler to understand the algorithm this way.

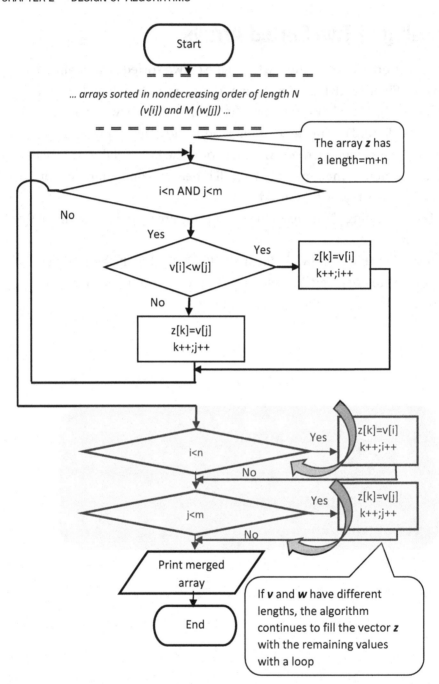

Figure 2-18. *Flow chart for the "merging of two sorted arrays" algorithm*

Suppose we have stored the following five numbers into a sorted array, v:

v[4]={14, 28, 49, 86, 94} and length n = 5

Suppose we have stored the following three numbers into a sorted array, w:

w[2]={3, 51, 80} and length m = 3

After initializing the variables (i = 0; j = 0; k = 0), the execution of the algorithm is shown in Table 2-12.

Table 2-12. *Merging of Two Sorted Arrays: Table of Values*

Iteration	i	j	k	i<n AND j<m	v[i]	w[j]	v[i]<w[j]	z[k]
1°	0	0	0	YES	14	3	NO	{3}
2°	0	1	1	YES	14	51	YES	{3, 14}
3°	1	1	2	YES	28	51	YES	{3, 14, 28}
4°	2	1	3	YES	49	51	YES	{3, 14, 28, 49}
5°	3	1	4	YES	86	51	NO	{3, 14, 28, 49, 51}
6°	3	2	5	YES	86	80	NO	{3, 14, 28, 49, 51, 80}
7°	3	3	6	NO	-		YES	{3, 14, 28, 49, 51, 80, 86}
8°	4	3	7			.	YES	{3, 14, 28, 49, 51, 80, 86, 94}
9°	5	3	8				NO	

This is the merged array:

z[7]={3, 14, 28, 49, 51, 80, 86, 94}

Reading Chars from a Text File

Finally, we will introduce how to read a data archive (a file or a database), which results in a relatively simple procedure, as it is based on the concept of *end of file* (EOF). EOF is a system keyword used by programming languages and is useful to exit a while loop. We will always analyze whether the file is empty or it has ended (meaning we have read all the characters in it) in the test of the while loop. Figure 2-19 illustrates the flow chart.

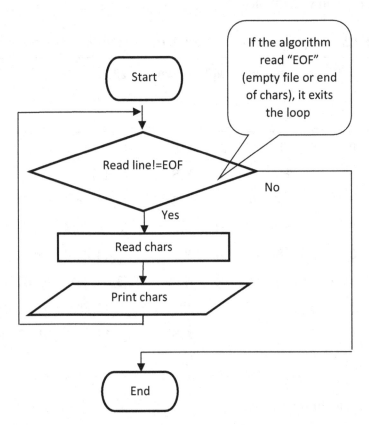

Figure 2-19. *Flow chart for "reading chars from a text file" algorithm*

This procedure is also used by the web programming languages for reading data archives from a database.

Functions and Subprograms

It is useful for programs to be read, shared, and easily modified, so they are usually divided into blocks (inserted in the same file or in different files) and linked to the main program (`main`). The individual blocks are called *subprograms*; they depend on the purpose and the programming language and often return a result (equal to a mathematical function). Examples are sort and search algorithms. A subprogram is called at a point of the main program (whose address is saved in the system stack), and then, after computation, the main program continues from the exact address saved in the stack, as shown in Figure 2-20.

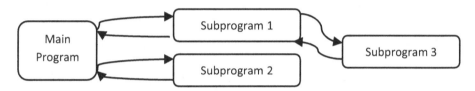

Figure 2-20. *Subprograms management*

The system must remember the place where the call was made so that it is possible to return to that exact point after the subprogram is complete. It is also necessary to remember local variables, processor registers, etc.

Working with a Stack

In this section, we will present a simple application of a subprogram. We will design a simple algorithm for a stack. Note that a *stack* is similar to an array, where the element in position 0 can be the bottom of the stack, while the top depends on the operation of `push`. The stack is a finite informative structure, while an array is an example of a limited informative structure, as shown in Figure 2-21 (similar to Figure 1-4 of Chapter 1).

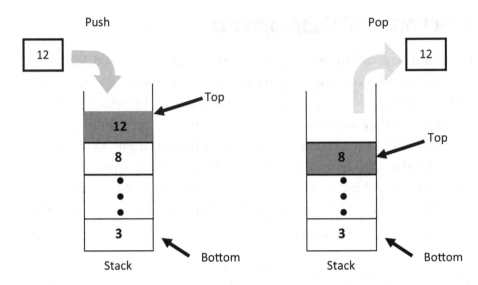

Figure 2-21. *Stack management: push and pop operations*

In this way, it is possible to create an array (for example, a stack s[10] of 10 elements), as depicted in Figure 2-22. It is important to save the elements in the right position of the array and set an index for the position of the top element.

The operations are as follows:

- **Push operation**: This inserts an element in the top of the stack.

- **Pop operation**: This removes an element from the top of the stack.

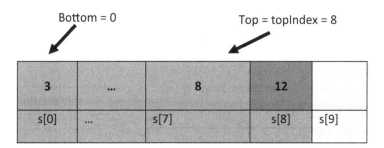

Figure 2-22. *Stack management with an array*

We need an index (named topIndex) that sets where the last inserted element is. It is equal to -1. In other words, the stack is empty and increases when an element is added. Therefore, it gives information about the stack's status. The bottom index is always equal to 0. The array values with an array index greater than topIndex are not significant. When topIndex is equal to the length of the array (MAX), the stack is *full*.

Therefore, we have to define a main program that sets the operations to do the following:

- Push
- Pop
- End program

The following are the three subprograms:

- Push
- Pop
- Print stack

Figure 2-23 illustrates the flow chart of the algorithm.

61

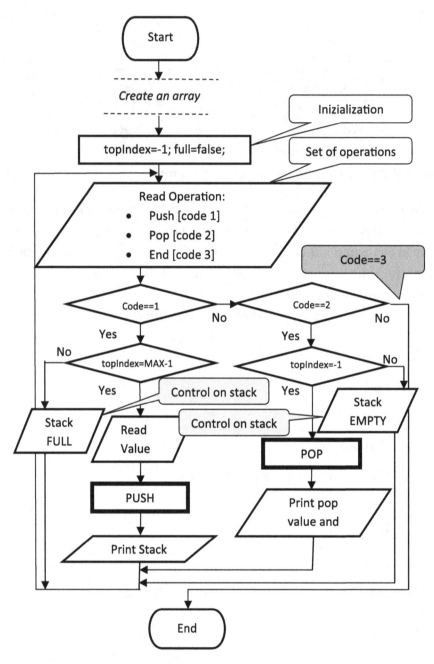

Figure 2-23. *Flow chart of the "stack management with an array" algorithm*

The push subprogram sets the following:

- `s[topIndex]=value;`

- `topIndex++;`

The pop subprogram sets the following:

- `popValue= s[topIndex];`

- `topIndex--;`

Finally, the print subprogram shows the stack.

Recursion

Recursion is the name for a process in which an algorithm invokes itself until the occurrence of the output condition. In other words, a subprogram calls itself before the termination of its own execution until the output condition. The addresses of the subprograms are set in the system stack.

The Factorial Function

An example of recursion is the factorial function of a positive integer that is usually defined in mathematics with the following:

$$\begin{cases} 0!=1; \\ n!=1*2*3*......*n-1*n; \text{for } n>0 \end{cases}.$$

The factorial is equal to 1 if N is equal to 0; otherwise, it is necessary to multiply N by the factorial of N-1, until N=0 or N=1.

If we want to use an iterative form, we use this:

```
if (N==0 OR N==1)
 then factorial =1
```

```
else
 for (i from 2 to N)
 factorial = factorial *i
```

If we want to use a recursive form, as depicted in Figure 2-24, we use this:

```
if (N==0 OR N==1)
  then factorial =1
else
  factorial (N) = N * factorial (N-1)
```

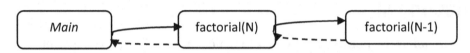

Figure 2-24. *Factorial management*

The Fibonacci Sequence

The Fibonacci sequence is a sequence of numbers defined by the following rule: "Every number after the first two is given by the sum of the two preceding ones." Therefore, the sequence is as follows:

$$1,1,2,3,5,8,13,21,34,55,89,144,233,377,610…$$

Each element of the Fibonacci sequence is calculated on the previous items of the same series.

It is usually defined in mathematics with the following:

$$\begin{cases} \text{fib}(2)=1; \\ \text{fib}(1)=1; \\ \text{fib}(n)=\text{fib}(n\ 1)+\text{fib}(n\ 2); \text{ for} n>2 \end{cases}$$

Specifically, to calculate the position of the *n* element, it is necessary to sum the two previous elements, i.e., the one in *n-2* position and the one in *n-1* position.

The assumption is that the initial values are both 1. Figure 2-25 illustrates this.

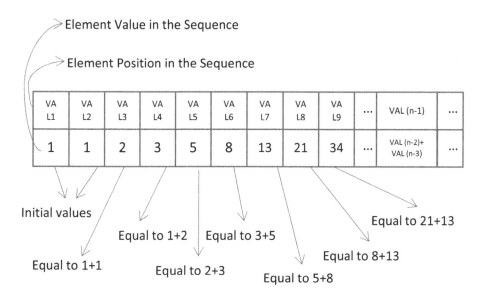

Figure 2-25. *The Fibonacci sequence*

If we suppose the calculation of fib(5), it is possible to count eight distinct calls at the same subprogram fib(k), as shown in Figure 2-26.

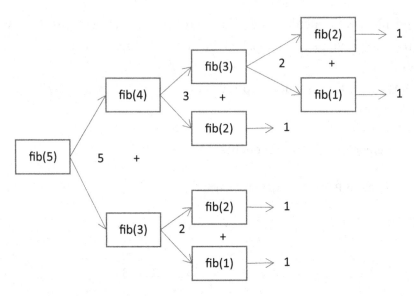

Figure 2-26. *The Fibonacci recursive calls*

In the simple schema shown in Figure 2-27, it is also possible to evaluate the memory allocation.

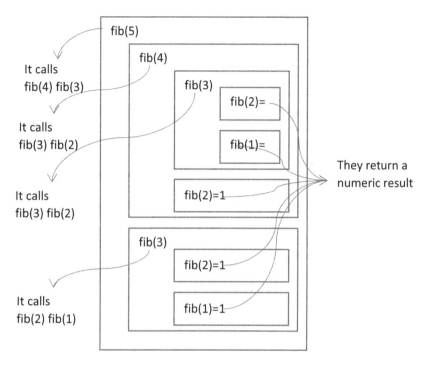

Figure 2-27. *The Fibonacci memory allocation*

If we wanted, we can draw a flow chart to explain the algorithm in a simpler way. It is possible to notice that the blocks in the gray shape are not formally structured, as depicted in Figure 2-28.

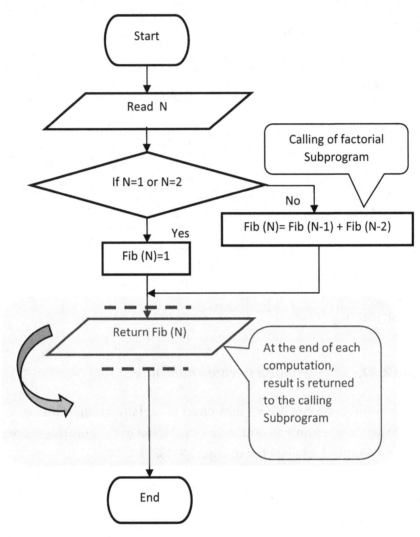

Figure 2-28. *The Fibonacci algorithm*

CHAPTER 3

Implementation of Algorithms in the C Programming Language

Algorithms are usually destined to be implemented as computer programs. A programming language offers a set of primitive, standard operators and rules. We will use these elements when writing our programs in C in this chapter.

The C language was born at Bell Labs. C is a useful language for developing applications, and it allows us to translate an algorithm into a program and to define functions. It is educationally interesting because it is a language still used, and it has many development environments (for example, we will use Dev-C++, which you can download for free). C is also easy to learn and produces efficient programs. Finally, the C language has a similar syntax to other important languages (derived from it), such as C++, Java, and JavaScript.

A C source file has the extension `.c`. Once the file is compiled, it generates an executable file with the same name as the source.

© Luciano Manelli 2020
L. Manelli, *Introducing Algorithms in C*, https://doi.org/10.1007/978-1-4842-5623-7_3

The source program usually has a section with the definitions of the library/file (introduced by the tag #include) and variables being used, as well as a section with the code (introduced by the tag main()). To make reading the program easier, you should indent the program that you are writing, as shown in the following example, where there are three levels (in this case, identified by the braces):

FIRST LEVEL{

> Indentation → **SECOND LEVEL{**

> > Indentation → **THIRD LEVEL{**
> > **}** closing braces of **THIRD LEVEL**

> > **}** closing braces of **SECOND LEVEL**

> **}** closing braces of **FIRST LEVEL**

In the next section, we will analyze the basic commands that will be used to develop the programs in this chapter.

C Code Fundamentals

Our programs will always start with the command #include <stdio.h>, which is a preprocessor command that tells a C compiler to include the stdio.h file before compilation. The main function where the program execution begins is indicated by the command main() (or int main()).

```
main(){
    /*
    our program
    */
}
```

The curly brackets open and close a set of code lines.

The lines in /*...*/ are comments in the program. Comments are important to explain the program and are ignored by the compiler when creating the executable.

Variables are locations in the computer's memory to store data, indicated by a unique name called an *identifier*.

It is important to choose a meaningful name for an identifier that is easy to understand and work on!

Constants are particular entities that cannot be changed during the execution of a program (also indicated by an identifier).

Finally, there are keywords that are the reserved words used in programming (such as int, void, main, and so on). The common development environments help you to identify the keywords and to write good code.

Fundamental/Primitive Types

Fundamental or primitive types are basic and simple data types used to specify a variable for storing data values. They include the following:

- Integer types

- Floating types

- Character types

Derived Types

Derived types are complex data types and usually constructed from primitive types. They include the following:

- Arrays

- Pointers

- Structures

71

Arrays

This data structure is used to store multiple values of the same type in a single variable. The syntax for declaring an array is as follows:

```
int exampleOfArrayOfInteger[100]; /* This sentence declares an
array of int*/
char exampleOfArrayOfChar[100]; /* This sentence declares an
array of char */
```

Pointers

Pointers are used to access the memory and manipulate the address of variables, so if var is a variable, then &var is the address in memory. A pointer variable is a special type of variable that holds a memory address rather than data. It is defined by a dereference operator (*), as shown in the following example:

```
FILE *fil;   /*fil is a pointer variable of type FILE*/
```

Structures

Structures group items of different types into a single type, as shown in the following example:

```
struct address{
      char city[15];
      int postal_code[5];
};
```

The Type void

The type void indicates that no value is available/returned.

Variable Declaration

The syntax for declaring a variable is as follows:

type variable_name;

Here are some examples:

```
int a;
float b; double f;
char c;
```

Boolean

Type Boolean (a type that stores a `true` or `false` value) is not defined as a primitive type. However, it can be an important data type used in decision blocks, so we simply will define a new type with the command `typedef`. The syntax is as follows:

```
typedef int bool; /*definition of a type bool*/
   #define true 1 /*true is 1*/
   #define false 0 /*false is 0*/
```

Arithmetic Operators

An operator specifies what is to be done to variables and constants. The following are the common mathematical operations:

- Addition or unary plus (+)

- Subtraction or unary minus (-)

- Multiplication (*)

- Division (/)

- Modulo division (%)

73

Relational Operators

The following are the relational operators:

- Greater than (>): 25 > 16 is TRUE

- Less than (<): 40 < 50 is TRUE

- Greater than or equal to (>=): 55 >= 55 is TRUE

- Less than or equal to (<=): 33 <= 44 is TRUE

- Equal to (==): 100 == 100 is TRUE; 7== 8 is FALSE

- Not equal to (!=): 7!= 8 is TRUE; 100 != 100 is FALSE

- AND (&&)

- OR (||)

- NOT (!)

Functions

Functions are blocks of code used to perform actions. They are usually called many times in the program but defined only once. Functions are also used to organize code, even if they are called just once in the program.

A function has a declaration that gives structural information, such as the return value (the value returned by the function and defined by a data type at the beginning of the function declaration) or the input parameters (input variables of the function passed inside the parentheses).

A function's code can be at the beginning of the program (before the main program that calls it) or at the end of the program. In the latter case, a prototype (a blueprint of the function that gives structural information) is required, because the main program must know about the presence of functions. The following is the syntax for declaring a prototype:

```
int multipleOfAReadValue (int value);
/* a function that returns a multiple of a read value */
...
```

The following is the syntax for creating a function:

```
int multipleOfAReadValue (int value){
/*
code
*/
}
```

Examples:

```
    float media (int a, int b)
    {
          return ((a+b)/2);
    }
    void swap (int *a, int *b)
    {
          int temp;
          temp =a;
          a=b;
          b= temp;
    }
```

Library Functions

A function available in C (in the library stdio.h) is printf(message), which displays on the screen a message from the program. Another function is scanf(), which reads from standard input.

Inside printf() there is, for example, a conversion format string, %d (for integer). If this conversion format string matches the argument, the values are correctly displayed.

The following are the conversion specifications for printf():

- %c: Character

- %s: String of characters

- %d or %i: Decimal integer

- %f: Floating-point number in decimal notation

- %u: Unsigned decimal integer

- %o: Octal integer

- %x: Hexadecimal integer, using lowercase

- %X: Hexadecimal integer, using uppercase

Statements

The sequence or statement represents a single instruction followed by a semicolon or a sequence of instructions delimited by two braces, { and }.

```
{
    instruction 1;
    instruction 2;
    instruction 3;
}
```

The if statement tests certain conditions (the result of the test can be true or false). If the evaluated expression is true, then *instruction 1* is executed (or a sequence of instructions in braces is executed). If the evaluated expression is false and if there is an alternative set of instructions (in this case *instruction 2*) identified by the else part, then *instruction 2* (or a sequence of instructions) is executed. The construct has the following syntax:

```
if (condition check)
            instruction 1;
    else /*alternative instruction*/
            instruction 2;
```

The switch statement tests the value of a variable and dispatches the execution to different code blocks depending on the result of the test. The evaluated expression is compared with the values of each case. If a case matches the expression value, then the instructions in the case block are executed (e.g., if expression matches value1, then *1-instructions* is executed). The break keyword breaks out of the case block; otherwise, the switch statement continues to test the value against the remaining tests, which is not normally what we want. Finally, the default keyword identifies a case block that defines a set of instructions that are executed if there is no case match. You can see that missing a break statement would lead to the default code running as well as the appropriate case statement. The construct has the following syntax:

```
switch( expression )
{
    case value1:
                1-instructions;
                break;
  ...
    case valueN:
                N-instructions;
                break;
    default:
                default-instructions;
                break;
}
```

Loops can execute a sequence of instructions, delimited by two braces, { and }, as long as a specified *condition check*, identified by the keyword while, is reached. The expression can be evaluated at the beginning of the loop or at the end of the loop. Note that in the first case (the while loop) the specified *condition* is checked before the execution of the instructions, while in the second case (the do-while loop), the *condition* is checked after the instructions are executed so will always run at least once.

- The while loop syntax, represented in Chapter 2 as the while loop, is as follows:

```
while (condition check)
        {
        instruction 1;
        instruction 2;
        instruction 3;
        }
```

- The do-while loop syntax, represented in Chapter 2 as the repeat loop, is as follows:

```
do
    {
        instruction 1;
        instruction 2;
        instruction 3;
    }
        while (condition check)
```

- The for loop is used when it is known exactly how many times the block of instructions in the loop will be executed. In this case, a smart expression is used, characterized by an *initial statement* executed one time before the block instructions, a *condition check* defined to exit the loop if it is evaluated to true, and an *increment* executed after the block of instructions has been executed.

```
for (initialization
    statement; condition check; increment)
    {
      instruction 1;
      instruction 2;
      instruction 3;
    }
```

Dev-C++ Environment

You can download the Dev-C++ environment at https://sourceforge.net/projects/orwelldevcpp/ for free, and it is compatible with different C standards. Then you can launch the executable file. It is a simple integrated development environment (IDE) that you can use to run all the examples contained in this book.

To be able to compile (and run) the examples, you only need to choose File ➤ New ➤ Source File, as shown in Figure 3-1, and then insert the C code (you can copy and paste the listings).

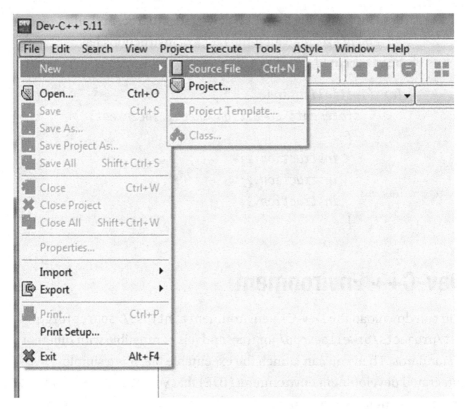

Figure 3-1. *The Dev-C++ environment, creating a new file*

To run the examples, you need to click the Execute button and then click Compile & Run. Before running the program, you will need to save the file. The default extension is .cpp and not .c, so you have to change the extension in order to save the file in the correct way. See Figure 3-2.

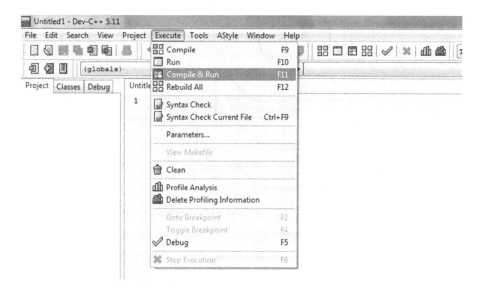

Figure 3-2. *The Dev-C++ environment, compiling and running an example*

C Programs

In the following sections, we will develop the programs of the algorithms explained in Chapter 2. Remember always to use an acceptable indentation style to make your code easier to read.

Sum of Three Numbers

This example highlights some basic elements of programming in C.

It might be interesting to revisit the flow chart of the algorithm, as shown in Figure 3-3.

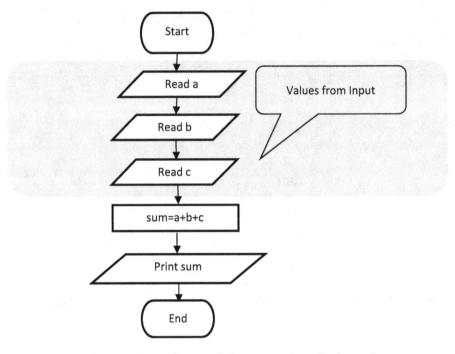

Figure 3-3. *Flow chart of "sum of three numbers" algorithm*

First, it is necessary to read an input value, as highlighted in the input blocks in the gray shape.

We are supposed to read three integer numbers, which is possible with the following code:

```
printf("Enter number a: ");
scanf("%d", &a);
```

The first command prints a message on the screen, and the second reads the input value from the keyboard (after pressing the Return key on the keyboard). It stores the value in a location addressed by the pointer &a. The input format is set with %d.

The following code sets the sum of the input values:

```
sum = a+b+c;
```

At the end, the sum is displayed with a decimal format.

```
printf("Sum: %d",sum);
```

It shows the value Sum (not its address like the function scanf). The output format is set with %d.

At the beginning of the program, there is the include command, which contains the declaration of the functions printf and scanf.

Finally, it is important to note that at the end of each code line there is a semicolon (;), which sets its end.

Source Program and Program Output

The C code is shown here:

```
#include <stdio.h>
int a,b,c,sum;

    main() {
        printf("Enter number a: ");
        scanf("%d",&a);

        printf("Enter number b: ");
        scanf("%d",&b);

        printf("Enter number c: ");
        scanf("%d",&c);

        sum = a+b+c;
        printf("Sum: %d",sum);
    }
```

Figure 3-4 shows the program output.

```
Enter number a: 2
Enter number b: 3
Enter number c: 4
Sum: 9
```

Figure 3-4. *Program output for "sum of three numbers"*

Sum of *n* Numbers in a Loop

In the "sum of *n* numbers in a loop" algorithm, it is possible to highlight the loop construct. You may want to revisit the flow chart of the algorithm, shown in Figure 2-8 of Chapter 2.

First, it is necessary to read N, i.e., the number of values to read.

```
printf("Enter how many number to add: ");
scanf("%d",&N);
```

The following code sets the sum to 0:

```
sum = 0;
```

Now, it is possible to study the three types of loop constructs shown in the gray input blocks of the following figures.

while Loop

Figure 3-5 shows the while loop. The blocks in the dashed line are the operations in the loop. The while command is identified with bold text, while the initialization (i=0) and the increment (i++) of i are part of the loop and are set in different lines of code, as you can see in the following listing:

```
i=0;
while (i<N){
```

84

```
   . . .
 i++;
}
```

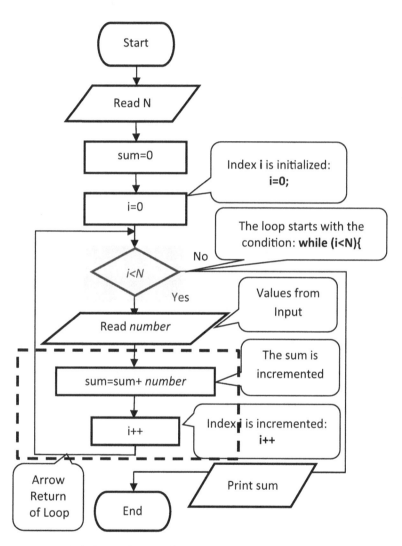

Figure 3-5. *while loop for the "sum of n numbers in a loop" algorithm*

for Loop

The for loop contains the initialization of index i, the test condition, and the index increment, as shown in Figure 3-6. The blocks in the dashed lines are the operations in the loop. The for command is identified with three gray shapes, and it is set in a line of code, as you can see in the following listing:

```
for (i=0; i<N; i++){
    ...
    }
```

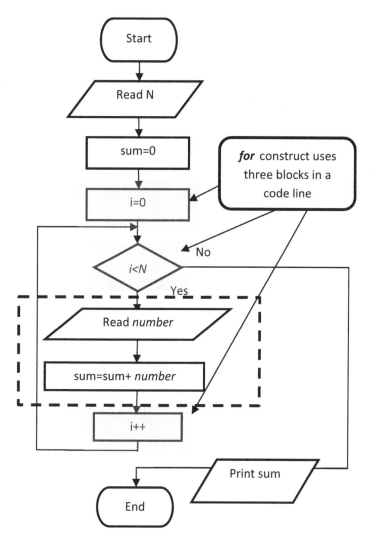

Figure 3-6. *for loop for the "sum of n numbers in a loop" algorithm*

do-while Loop

Figure 3-7 shows the do-while loop. The blocks in the dashed lines are the operations in the loop. The do-while command is identified with a gray shape, and it is at the end of the loop block, while the initialization (i=0) and the increment (i++) of i are part of the loop and are set in different lines of code, as you can see in the following listing:

```
i=0;
do
{
    ...
   i++;
} while (i<N);
```

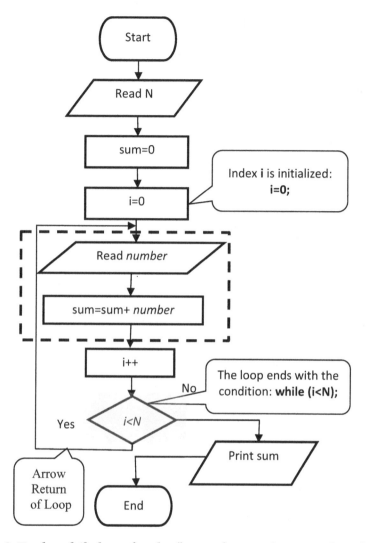

Figure 3-7. *do-while loop for the "sum of n numbers in a loop" algorithm*

Source Program of the while loop

The C code of the while loop, with some indentation, is shown here:

```c
#include <stdio.h>
   int N;
   int i;
   int sum;
   int number;

   main() {
   printf("Enter how many number to add: ");
   scanf("%d",&N);

   i=0;
   while (i<N){
      printf(" Enter number %d:",i+1);
      scanf("%d", &number);
      sum = sum + number;
      i++;
   }
   printf("Sum: %d",sum);
}
```

Source Program of the for loop

The C code of the for loop, with some indentation, is shown here:

```c
#include <stdio.h>
   int N;
   int i;
   int sum;
   int number;
```

```
main() {
printf("Enter how many number to add: ");
scanf("%d",&N);

for (i=0;i<N;i++){
    printf(" Enter number %d:",i+1);
    scanf("%d", &number);
    sum = sum + number;
 }
 printf("Sum: %d",sum);
 }
```

Source Program for the do-while Loop

The C code of the do-while loop, with some indentation, is shown here:

```
#include <stdio.h>
    int N;
    int i;
    int sum;
    int number

    main() {
    printf("Enter how many number to add: ");
    scanf("%d",&N);

    i=0;
    do{
        printf(" Enter number %d:",i+1);
        scanf("%d", &number);
        sum = sum + number;
        i++;
    } while (i<N);
    printf("Sum: %d",sum);
}
```

Program Output

Figure 3-8 shows the program output, which is the same for the three types of loops.

```
Enter how many number to add: 3
 Enter number 1:1
 Enter number 2:3
 Enter number 3:4
Sum: 8
_____
```

Figure 3-8. *Program output for "sum of n numbers in a loop"*

Note that the while loops based on the test of an index i need the increment of the index (i.e., i++). This avoids an infinite number of cycles. Try to comment out the command and see the error for yourself!

Storing Numbers Within an Array

This example creates an array of length N and assigns values to it. We will assume that N is variable, but its max is 100! In this code, we will see how to create an array in the C language.

First, there is the definition of an array of 100 elements.

```c
int arr[100];
```

Then, it is possible to define two types of loops for uploading the numbers in the array.

You can use the while loop, as shown here:

```c
i=0;
while (i<N){
   printf(" Enter number in position %d:",i);
   scanf("%d", &arr[i]);
   i++;
}
```

You can use the for loop, as shown here:

```
for (i=0; i<N; i++){
   printf(" Enter number in position %d:",i);
   scanf("%d", &arr[i]);
}
```

Notice that, in this case, the for loop is simpler than the while loop.

Source Program and Program Output

The C code is shown here:

```
#include <stdio.h>
   int N;
   int i;
   int arr[100];

   main() {
   printf("Enter array length (max 100): ");
       scanf("%d",&N);
       i=0;
       while (i<N){
          printf(" Enter number in position %d:",i);
          scanf("%d", &arr[i]);
          i++;
       }
   /*
   //Alternative for loop
      for (i=0; i<N; i++){
        printf(" Enter number in position %d:",i);
        scanf("%d", &arr[i]);
    }
   */
```

```
    printf("Numbers of the array:");
    for(i=0;i<N;i++) {
      printf("%d;", arr[i]);
    }
  }
```

Figure 3-9 shows the program output.

```
Enter array length (max 100): 2
 Enter number in position 0:1
 Enter number in position 1:45
Numbers of the array:1;45;
-----------------------------------
```

Figure 3-9. *Program output of "storing numbers within an array"*

Array Exercise

In this exercise, the elements are stored in an array of length N, and the percentage and the sum are calculated.

Specifically, the result elements are printed in reverse order. It is sufficient to vary the loop conditions, starting from the last index (N-1) to the first index (0), with step -1.

Now we define and use floating input, as shown here:

float arr[50], p, sum=0

The percentage is defined in a mathematical way as follows:

arr[i]=((arr[i]/**100.0)*p**);

Source Program and Program Output

The C code is shown here:

```c
#include <stdio.h>
int N, i;
float arr[50], p, sum=0;
main() {
 p=0;
 printf("Enter percentage : \n");
 scanf("%f",&p); //percentage of 50%

 printf("Enter array length(max 50):\n");
 scanf("%d", &N);

 for (i=0; i<N; i++){
     printf("Enter number in position %d:",i);
     scanf("%f", & arr[i]);
 }

 for(i=0;i<N;i++) {
   arr[i]=(( arr[i]/100.0)*p);
   sum = sum + arr[i];
 }
   printf("Array with elements in reverse order: \n ");
 for(i=N-1;i>=0;i--) {
   printf("%f \n", arr[i]);
 }

 printf("Sum = %f", sum);
}
```

Figure 3-10 shows the program output.

```
Enter percentage :
30
Enter array length(max 50):
3
Enter number in position 0:10
Enter number in position 1:20
Enter number in position 2:30
Array with elements in reverse order:
9.000000
6.000000
3.000000
Sum = 18.000000
```

Figure 3-10. *Program output of "exercise with an array"*

Converting a Decimal Number to a Binary Number

This example will show an algorithmic solution to convert a decimal to a binary.

First, the array is initialized, and each element is set to 0. Then the decimal input is read and controlled (0<N<255).

Finally, a while loop sets the reminders in the array elements (the first reminder in v[0], the second one in v[1], etc.) and calculates the quotient (N=N/2) as a new input value of the loop (it is the new value to be divided by 2).

When the quotient equals 0 (N==0), the loop ends.

It is interesting to revisit the algorithm, as shown in Figure 3-11.

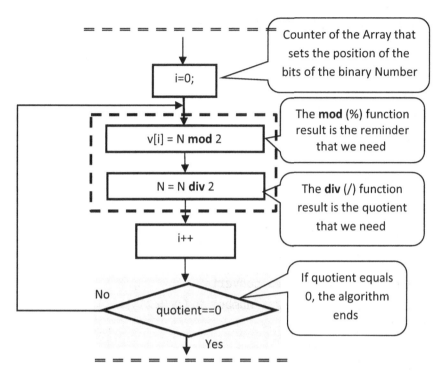

Figure 3-11. *Flow chart of "converting a decimal number to a binary number" algorithm*

Note that for this example, the condition that is used to exit the loop is based on a test on the quotient (identified with a gray shape), while the use of the increment of an index i is used for storing the remainders in the array (that represents the binary number).

In the algorithm, two mathematical functions are used (the two blocks in the dashed lines).

- The mod function that returns the remainder after the division of two numbers: N%2 in the C language

- The div function that returns the quotient after the division of two numbers: N/2 in the C language

Source Program and Program Output

The C code is shown here:

```c
#include <stdio.h>
int N;
int i;
int v[8];
int quotient;

main() {
  //initializing an array
  for (i=0; i<8; i++) v[i]=0;

  //reading the number to convert
  printf("Enter an integer number N (0<N<255): ");
  scanf("%d",&N);
  if (N<0  ||  N>255)  {
    while (N<0 || N>255){
        printf("Enter an integer number N (0<N<255): ");
        scanf("%d",&N);
    }
  }

  i=0;
  while (N!=0) {
    v[i]=N%2;
    //optional printing of the reminder = v[i]
    printf("v[%d]:%d;\n", i, v[i]);
    //N become the reminder
    N=N/2;
```

```
    //optional printing of the quotient
    printf("quotient:%d;\n", N);
    i++;
  }

  printf("Result array:\n");
  for(i=7;i>=0;i--) {
    printf("%d", v[i]);
  }
}
```

Figure 3-12 shows the program output. The test is done also on two numbers under (-48) and over (900) the range (0<N<255).

```
Enter an integer number N (0<N<255): -48
Enter an integer number N (0<N<255): 900
Enter an integer number N (0<N<255): 56
v[0]:0;
quotient:28;
v[1]:0;
quotient:14;
v[2]:0;
quotient:7;
v[3]:1;
quotient:3;
v[4]:1;
quotient:1;
v[5]:1;
quotient:0;
Result array:
00111000
```

Figure 3-12. *Program output of "converting a decimal number to a binary number"*

Maximum/Minimum Search

In this example, the elements are stored in an array of length N. There are two comparisons with the maximum and minimum value candidates, which are set equal to the first element of the array, as we can see in the following piece of code:

```
min=arr[0];
max=arr[0];
```

If an element of the array is smaller than the minimum, the minimum is set equal to that element. If an element of the array is bigger than the maximum, the maximum is set equal to that element, as we can see in the following piece of code:

```
if (arr[i]<min)
      min=arr[i];
  else if(arr[i]>max)
      max=arr[i];
```

Source Program and Program Output

The C code is shown here:

```
#include <stdio.h>
int min;
int max;
int N;
int i;
int arr[100];

main() {

printf("Enter array length (max 100): ");
      scanf("%d",&N);
```

```
        i=0;
        while (i<N){
            printf(" Enter number in position %d:",i);
            scanf("%d", &arr[i]);
            i++;
    }
min=arr[0];
max=arr[0];
for( i=1; i<N; i=i+1)
    {
      if (arr[i]<min)
          min=arr[i];
      else if(arr[i]>max)
          max=arr[i];
    }
printf("max: %d \n", max);
printf("min: %d \n", min);
    }
```

Figure 3-13 shows the program output.

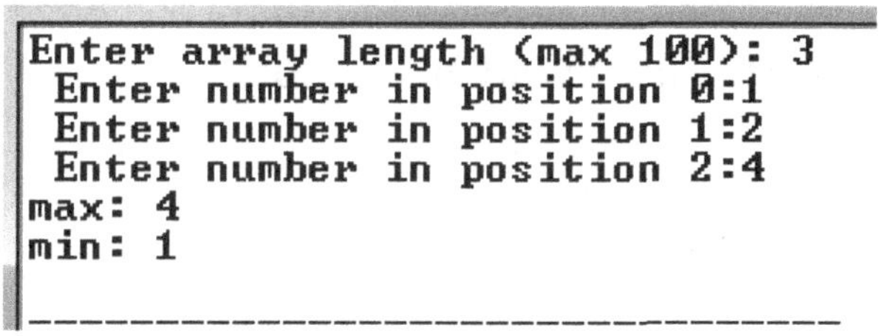

```
Enter array length (max 100): 3
 Enter number in position 0:1
 Enter number in position 1:2
 Enter number in position 2:4
max: 4
min: 1
_____
```

Figure 3-13. *Program output of "maximum/minimum search"*

Linear/Sequential Search

In this example, the elements are stored in an array of length N. The variable search_key contains the value read from input. If the searching value is found, it is possible to exit the loop, so a Boolean variable is defined (through the typedef command), as shown in the following listing:

```
typedef int bool;
  #define true 1
  #define false 0
```

The input values are as follows:

- The array length N

- The elements of the array arr[i]

- The search_key we want to search for in the array

The variable found is set to false at the beginning of the loop.

```
found=false;
```

At the end of the program, if the value found is false, in other words, the searched value was not found, a message is displayed.

Source Program and Program Output

The C code is shown here:

```
#include <stdio.h>
  int N;
  int i;
  int search_key;
  typedef int bool;
    #define true 1
    #define false 0
```

```c
      bool found;
      int arr[100];
main() {
   printf("Enter array length (max 100): ");
   scanf("%d",&N);
   i=0;
   while (i<N){
      printf(" Enter number in position %d:",i);
      scanf("%d", &arr[i]);
      i++;
   }
   printf("Enter the search_key: ");
   scanf("%d",&search_key);

   found=false;
   for(i=0; i<N && found==false; i++) {
     if (arr[i]==search_key) {
            found =true;
            printf("search key is in position: %d \n",i);
     }
   }
  if (found ==false) {
    printf("the search key was not found in the array");
    }
}
```

Figure 3-14 shows the program output for a positive search.

```
Enter array length (max 100): 5
 Enter number in position 0:28
 Enter number in position 1:14
 Enter number in position 2:61
 Enter number in position 3:49
 Enter number in position 4:3
Enter the search_key: 49
search key is in position: 3
_____
```

Figure 3-14. *Program output of positive "linear/sequential search"*

Figure 3-15 shows the program output for a negative search.

```
Enter array length (max 100): 5
 Enter number in position 0:28
 Enter number in position 1:14
 Enter number in position 2:61
 Enter number in position 3:49
 Enter number in position 4:3
Enter the search_key: 50
the search key was not found in the array
_____
```

Figure 3-15. *Program output of negative "linear/sequential search"*

Binary Search

In the following algorithm, the elements are stored in an array sorted in nondecreasing order of length N. The variable search_key contains the value read from input.

Then, before the loop, the indexes are set.

```
lft=0;
rig=N-1;
pos=-1;
```

The loop continues until the search key is found (in other words, the variable pos changes value) or the loop condition sets the end of the array, as shown in the following code:

```
while (lft<=rig && pos==-1)
```

Note that the conditions that are used to exit the loop are not based on a test of the increment of an index i.

At the end of the program, if the variable pos is *-1*, in other words, the searched value was not found, a message is displayed.

Source Program and Program Output

The C code is shown here:

```
#include <stdio.h>
    int N,i;
    int lft, rig, mdl, pos;
    int search_key;
    int arr[100];

  main() {
  printf("Enter array length (max 100): ");
    scanf("%d",&N);
     i=0;
     while (i<N){
       printf("Enter number in position %d:",i);
       scanf("%d", &arr[i]);
       i++;
     }
  printf("Enter the search_key: ");
  scanf("%d",&search_key);

  lft=0;
  rig=N-1;
```

```
pos=-1;
while(lft<=rig && pos==-1)
{
    mdl=(lft+rig+1)/2;
    if(arr[mdl]== search_key)
         pos=mdl;
    else
    {
        if(search_key<arr[mdl])
            rig=mdl-1;
        else
            lft=mdl+1;
    }
}
if(pos!=-1)
    printf("search key is in position: %d \n", pos);
else
    printf("the search key was not found in the array");
}
```

Figure 3-16 shows the program output for a positive search (search_key=75).

```
Enter array length (max 100): 8
Enter number in position 0:3
Enter number in position 1:14
Enter number in position 2:28
Enter number in position 3:49
Enter number in position 4:61
Enter number in position 5:75
Enter number in position 6:81
Enter number in position 7:94
Enter the search_key: 75
search key is in position: 5
_____
```

Figure 3-16. *Program output of positive "binary search"*

Figure 3-17 shows the program output for a negative search (search_key=50).

```
Enter array length (max 100): 8
Enter number in position 0:3
Enter number in position 1:14
Enter number in position 2:28
Enter number in position 3:49
Enter number in position 4:61
Enter number in position 5:75
Enter number in position 6:81
Enter number in position 7:94
Enter the search_key: 50
the search key was not found in the array
------------------------------------------
```

Figure 3-17. *Program output of negative "binary search"*

Bubble Sort

In the following algorithm, the variables N, i, j, temp, and arr[] are initialized, and the elements are stored in an array of orderable elements of length N. It is important to note that this is the first example where there are two loops.

- An external loop that scans all elements of the array

  for(i=0; i<N; i++) {

  ...

  }

- An internal loop that analyzes the piece of array interested in researching the smallest element to set at the top of the array

  for(j=N-1; j>i; j--) {

  ...

  }

In this case, there is a swap operation whenever the test block `arr[j]` `<arr[j-1]` is true.

```
if(arr[j]<arr[j-1]) {
        temp=arr[j];
        arr[j]=arr[j-1];
        arr[j-1]= temp;
    }
```

The comparison always starts from the end of the array (j=N-1), and it ends at the first not-ordered element (j>i).

At the end, the sorted array is displayed.

Source Program and Program Output

The C code is shown here:

```
#include <stdio.h>
    int N,i,j;
    int temp;
    int arr[100];

main() {
    printf("Enter array length (max 100): ");
    scanf("%d",&N);
    i=0;
        while (i<N){
            printf(" Enter number in position %d:",i);
            scanf("%d", &arr[i]);
            i++;
        }

        for(i=0;i<N;i++) {
            for(j=N-1;j>i; j--) {
```

```
            if(arr[j]<arr[j-1]) {
               temp=arr[j];
               arr[j]=arr[j-1];
               arr[j-1]= temp;
            }
         }
      }
      printf(" Sorted array:\n");
      for(i=0;i<N;i++)
         printf("%d\n",arr[i]);
}
```

Figure 3-18 shows the program output.

```
Enter array length (max 100): 6
 Enter number in position 0:28
 Enter number in position 1:14
 Enter number in position 2:61
 Enter number in position 3:49
 Enter number in position 4:3
 Enter number in position 5:1
 Sorted array:
1
3
14
28
49
61
_____
```

Figure 3-18. *Program output of "bubble sort"*

Selection Sort

In the following algorithm, the variables N, i, j, imin, temp, and arr[] are
initialized, and the elements are stored in an array of orderable elements of
length N. It is important to note that in this example there are two loops.

- An external loop that scans all elements of the array

```
for(i=0; i<N; i++) {
...
}
```

- An internal loop that analyzes the piece of array interested in researching the smallest index

```
for(j=i+1;j<N;j++) {
    if(arr[j]<arr[imin])
        imin=j;
}
```

In this case, the imin is searched, and it is set to the current value of j if the block arr[j] <arr[j-1] is true.

At the end of the internal loop there is the swap between the two elements of the array arr[i] (where there will be the smallest value) and arr[imin] (where there currently is the smallest value identified by the just found index imin).

```
temp=arr[i];
arr[i]=arr[imin];
arr[imin]=temp;
```

The comparison always starts from the first not-ordered element (j=i+1), and it ends at the end of the array (j<N).

At the end, the sorted array is displayed.

Source Program and Program Output

The C code is shown here:

```
#include <stdio.h>
    int N,i,j;
    int imin,temp;
```

```c
int arr[100];

main() {
 printf("Enter array length(max 100): ");
 scanf("%d",&N);
  i=0;
  while (i<N){
       printf(" Enter number in position %d:",i);
       scanf("%d", &arr[i]);
       i++;
  }
    for(i=0;i<N-1;i++) {
       imin=i;

       for(j=i+1;j<N;j++) {
          if(arr[j]<arr[imin])
               imin=j;
       }

       temp=arr[i];
       arr[i]=arr[imin];
       arr[imin]=temp;
    }

printf(" Sorted array:\n");
   for(i=0;i<N;i++)
       printf("%d \n",arr[i]) ;
}
```

Figure 3-19 shows the program output.

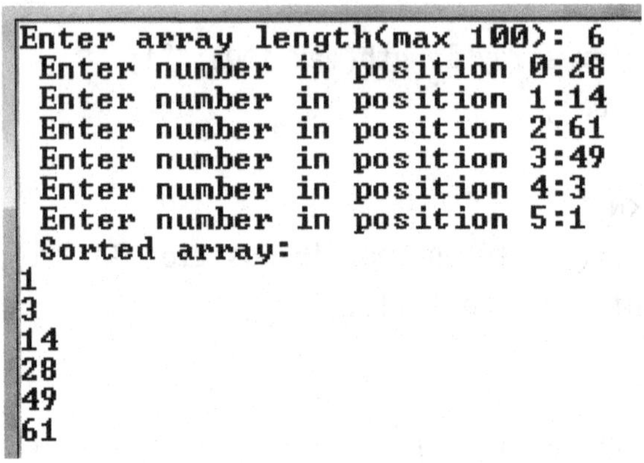

```
Enter array length(max 100): 6
 Enter number in position 0:28
 Enter number in position 1:14
 Enter number in position 2:61
 Enter number in position 3:49
 Enter number in position 4:3
 Enter number in position 5:1
 Sorted array:
1
3
14
28
49
61
```

Figure 3-19. *Program output of "selection sort"*

Note that by inserting some display instructions into the internal loop, it is possible to have a sort of log that explains the evolution of the sorting algorithm, as shown in Figure 3-20.

```
Enter array length(max 100): 6
 Enter number in position    arr[0]:28
 Enter number in position    arr[1]:14
 Enter number in position    arr[2]:61
 Enter number in position    arr[3]:49
 Enter number in position    arr[4]:3
 Enter number in position    arr[5]:1

 imin = 5
 arr[0]:1
 arr[1]:14
 arr[2]:61
 arr[3]:49
 arr[4]:3
 arr[5]:28
 imin = 4
 arr[0]:1
 arr[1]:3
 arr[2]:61
 arr[3]:49
 arr[4]:14
 arr[5]:28
 imin = 4
 arr[0]:1
 arr[1]:3
 arr[2]:14
 arr[3]:49
 arr[4]:61
 arr[5]:28
 imin = 5
 arr[0]:1
 arr[1]:3
 arr[2]:14
 arr[3]:28
 arr[4]:61
 arr[5]:49
 imin = 5
 arr[0]:1
 arr[1]:3
 arr[2]:14
 arr[3]:28
 arr[4]:49
 arr[5]:61
```

Figure 3-20. *Program output of "selection sort log"*

It is possible to use the previous listing with the following code lines highlighted in gray:

```
for(i=0;i<N-1;i++) {
    imin=i;
    for(j=i+1;j<N;j++) {
        if(arr[j]<arr[imin])
            imin=j;
    }
    printf("\n imin = %d ",imin) ;
    temp=arr[i];
    arr[i]=arr[imin];
    arr[imin]=temp;
    for(k=0;k<N;k++)
    printf(" \n arr[%d]:%d ",k,arr[k]) ;
}
```

Merging of Two Sorted Arrays

In this algorithm, the variables N, M, i, j, and k, as well as the arrays v, w, and z, are initialized, and the elements are stored in the two arrays sorted in nondecreasing order of lengths N and M. The merged array (z) is sorted in nondecreasing order and is of length N+M.

Note that for this example, the main loop is characterized by a complex for construct with three initializations and two conditions, as shown in the following code (highlighted in gray):

```
for (i=0,j=0,k=0; i<N && j<M;k++) {
    if(v[i]<w[j]) {
        z[k]=v[i];
        i++;
    } else {
```

```
    z[k]=w[j];
    j++;
  }
}
```

At the end, the final array is filled by the bigger array, and it is displayed.

Source Program and Program Output

The C code is shown here:

```
#include <stdio.h>
    int N, M,i,j,k;
    int v[100];
    int w[100];
    int z[200];

main() {
        printf("Enter array length of v (max 100): ");
        scanf("%d",&N);
        i=0;
        while (i<N){
          printf(" Enter number in position %d:",i);
          scanf("%d", &v[i]);
          i++;
        }

        printf("Enter array length of w (max 100): ");
        scanf("%d",&M);
        j=0;
        while (j<M){
            printf(" Enter number in position %d:",j);
            scanf("%d", &w[j]);
```

```c
        j++;
      }

    for (i=0,j=0,k=0;i<N && j<M;k++) {
      if(v[i]<w[j]) {
        z[k]=v[i];
        i++;
      } else {
        z[k]=w[j];
        j++;
      }
    }

    if (j<M) {
     while(j<M) {
      z[k]=w[j];
      k++;j++;
     }
    } else
       if (i<N)
       {
         while(i<N) {
           z[k]=v[i];
           k++;i++;
         }
       }

  printf(" Merged array (array z):\n");
  for(k=0;k<M+N;k++) {
     printf("number in position %d: %d\n",k,z[k]);
  }
}
```

Figure 3-21 shows the program output.

```
Enter array length of v (max 100): 5
 Enter number in position 0:14
 Enter number in position 1:28
 Enter number in position 2:49
 Enter number in position 3:86
 Enter number in position 4:94
Enter array length of w (max 100): 3
 Enter number in position 0:3
 Enter number in position 1:51
 Enter number in position 2:80
 Merged array (array z):
number in position 0:  3
number in position 1:  14
number in position 2:  28
number in position 3:  49
number in position 4:  51
number in position 5:  80
number in position 6:  86
number in position 7:  94

_____
```

Figure 3-21. *Program output of "merging of two sorted arrays"*

Functions and Subprograms

In Chapter 2, we learned that programs are usually divided into blocks called *subprograms* or *functions* and inserted into the same file or in different files, linked to the main program (main).

The individual blocks work on parameters passed in different ways. In the following listing, there is an example of the two main ways to pass arguments.

- **By value**: A copy of the value in memory is passed, and the function operates on its copy. In this case, the original value is not affected by the changes.

- **By address**: The address of the value in memory is passed, so the function parameter must be a pointer, and the function operates on the original value.

It is important to notice the function prototypes (or interfaces) defined before the main declaration, which allow the functions to be used before they are defined, as shown in the following code:

```
int sumValue(int val1,int val2);
int sumAddress(int *val1,int *val2);
```

Source Program and Program Output

The C code is shown here:

```
#include <stdio.h>
//variable
int a,b,result1,result2;
//by value
int sumValue(int val1,int val2);
//by address
int sumAddress(int *val1,int *val2);

main()
{

printf("Enter a: ");
scanf("%d",&a);
printf("Enter b: ");
scanf("%d",&b);

result1 = sumValue(a,b);
printf("Passing an argument by value: %d,%d \n",a,b);
printf("sumValue: %d\n", result1);

result2 = sumAddress(&a,&b);
printf("Passing an argument by address: %d,%d \n",a,b);
printf("sumValue: %d\n", result2);
}
```

```
/*by value*/
int sumValue(int val1,int val2)
{
return(val1+val2);
}
/*by address*/
int sumAddress(int *val1,int *val2)
{
return(*val1+*val2);
}
```

In this case, the result is the same.

Figure 3-22 shows the program output.

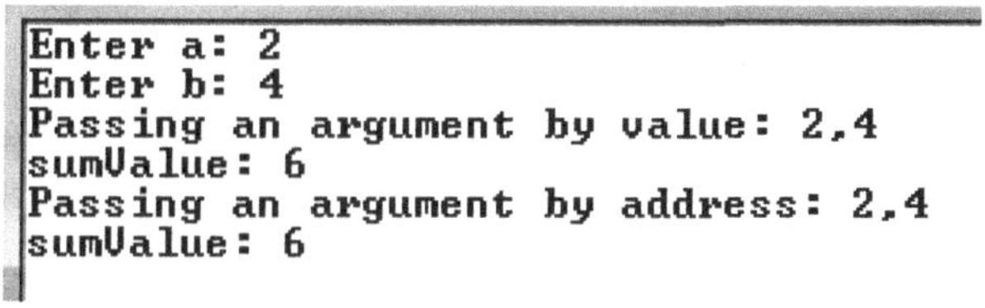

Figure 3-22. *Program output of first sum example*

In the following code, an input value is modified in two ways by adding a constant (5):

```
#include <stdio.h>
//variable
int a,result1,result2;
//by value
int modValue(int val1);
//by address
int modAddress(int *val1);
```

```
main()
{

printf("Enter a: ");
scanf("%d",&a);

result1 = modValue(a);
printf("Passing an argument by value: %d \n",a);
printf("modValue: %d\n", result1);

result2 = modAddress(&a);
printf("Passing an argument by address: %d \n",a);
printf("modValue: %d\n", result2);
}

/*by value*/
int modValue(int val1)
{
        val1=val1+5;
 return(val1);
}
/*by address*/
int modAddress(int *val1)
{
 *val1=*val1+5;
 return(*val1);
 }
```

In this case, the result is different, because in the second function the original value a is also modified (8), while in the first function only the copy is modified; in fact, the value a is the same (3), as shown in Figure 3-23.

```
Enter a: 3
Passing an argument by value: 3
modValue: 8
Passing an argument by address: 8
modValue: 8
```

Figure 3-23. *Program output of the second sum example*

Working with a Text File

In this program, we will use void return type functions because they do not return a value. Two functions (read and write) are declared, as shown in the following code:

```
void read(FILE *in,char testo[M]) ;
void write (char testo[M]);
```

In main, a variable FILE is defined as a pointer.

The command fopen allows us to open the file; it is in the library stdio.h. Once the file is opened, it is read, as an array of chars, with function fscanf, and then it is printed until the end of the file has been reached through the control of another test function, i.e., feof.

Source Program and Program Output

The C code is shown here:

```
#include <stdio.h>
int M=100;
void read(FILE *in,char textFile[M]) ;
void write (char textFile[M]);

main(){
FILE *fil;
char textFile[M];
fil = fopen("dat.txt","r");
```

121

```
printf("file of char:\n");
while (!feof(fil)){
read (fil,textFile);
write (textFile) ;
}
}
void read (FILE *in,char textFile[M]){
fscanf(in,"%s",textFile);
}
void write (char textFile[M]){
printf("%s\n",textFile) ;
}
```

In the file there is the following content, as you can also see in Figure 3-24:

Hello World!

This is your book!

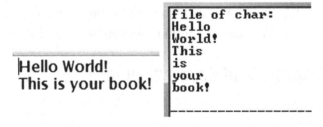

Figure 3-24. *Program output of "working with a text file"*

Working with a Stack

In this program, we will use three functions (push, pop, and print). The main loop is in an external loop that is used to present the menu at the end of each operation.

Note that in this case the program uses the do-while loop. In fact, at first, an options menu is presented, so the operation (push or pop) depends on the choice.

An array is used to represent the stack, with the definition of a top index. Note that in this example there are three functions.

- Function push: First it increments the pointer, and then it inserts a value into the stack, i.e., in the array, as highlighted in gray in the following listing:

```c
void push (int stack[], int item)
{
  topIndex++;
  stack [topIndex] = item;
}
```

- Function pop: First it reads the element in the stack, and then it decrements the pointer, as highlighted in gray in the following listing:

```c
int pop (int stack[])
{
 int ret;
 ret = stack [topIndex];
 topIndex--;
 return ret;
}
```

- Function display: First it controls that the stack is not empty (i.e., topIndex is different from -1), and then it prints the stack. It is used at the end of each operation (push or pop).

Note that in this example the functions are defined before the main code, so we do not need the use of the function prototypes.

Source Program and Program Output

The C code is shown here:

```c
#include <stdio.h>
#define MAX 50
int topIndex;

// PUSH function
void push (int stack[], int item)
{
        topIndex++;
        stack [topIndex] = item;
}

//POP function
int pop (int stack[])
{
    int ret;
        ret = stack [topIndex];
        topIndex--;
    return ret;
}

//DISPLAY function
void display (int stack[])
{
    int i;
    printf ("\nStack: ");
    if (topIndex == -1)
      printf ("empty");
    else
    {
      for (i=topIndex; i>=0; --i)
```

```
            printf ("\n-------\n|%d    |\n------- ",stack[i]);
    }
    printf ("\n");
}
//Main
void main()
{
    int stack [MAX], item;
    int choiceStack;
    topIndex = -1;

    do
    {
      do
      {
        //main menu
        printf ("\nChoose Operation:\n");
        printf ("\n1.Push");
        printf ("\n2.Pop");
        printf ("\n3-End Program\n");
        scanf  ("%d", &choiceStack);

        if (choiceStack<1 || choiceStack>3)
        printf ("\nInvalid Choice, Try again\n");
        }
      while (choiceStack<1 || choiceStack>3);

      switch (choiceStack)
      {
        case 1:
        if (topIndex == MAX-1) printf ("\nStack is FULL\n");
        else{
            printf ("\nEnter the Element to be pushed: \n");
```

```
            scanf  ("%d", &item);
            push (stack, item);
            display (stack);
            }
            break;

        case 2:
        if (topIndex == -1) printf ("\nStack is EMPTY\n");
        else
        {
            item = pop (stack);
            printf ("\nThe Popped item is: %d",item);
            display (stack);
        }

    break;

    default:
    printf ("\nEND OF EXECUTION\n");
    }
 }
while (choiceStack != 3);
}
```

Figure 3-25 shows the program output when a wrong value is typed. Figure 3-26 shows the program output of push (1) and pop (2) operations and the end (3) of the execution.

```
Choose Operation:

1.Push
2.Pop
3.End Program
23

Invalid Choice, Try again
```

Figure 3-25. *Program output of controlling an input parameter*

```
Choose Operation:

1.Push
2.Pop
3.End Program
23

Invalid Choice, Try again

Choose Operation:

1.Push
2.Pop
3.End Program
1

Enter the Element to be pushed:
12

Stack:
-------
|12   |
-------

Choose Operation:

1.Push
2.Pop
3.End Program
1

Enter the Element to be pushed:
23

Stack:
-------
|23   |
-------
-------
|12   |
-------

Choose Operation:

1.Push
2.Pop
3.End Program
2

The Popped item is: 23
Stack:
-------
|12   |
-------

Choose Operation:

1.Push
2.Pop
3.End Program
3

END OF EXECUTION
```

Figure 3-26. *Program output of pushing and popping an integer*

If the size of the array is two elements (#define MAX 2), when we try to insert a third element, the program shows a warning, as shown in Figure 3-27.

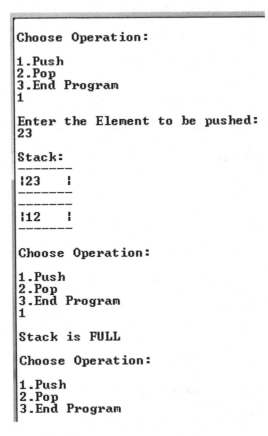

```
Choose Operation:

1.Push
2.Pop
3.End Program
1

Enter the Element to be pushed:
23

Stack:
_____
!23   !
_____
_____
!12   !
_____

Choose Operation:

1.Push
2.Pop
3.End Program
1

Stack is FULL

Choose Operation:

1.Push
2.Pop
3.End Program
```

Figure 3-27. *Program output: the stack is full*

Finally, if we try to pop an element when the stack is empty, the program shows a warning; see Figure 3-28.

```
Choose Operation:

1.Push
2.Pop
3.End Program
2

Stack is EMPTY

Choose Operation:

1.Push
2.Pop
3.End Program
```

Figure 3-28. *Program output: the stack is empty*

Recursive Algorithm: Factorial Function

Let's discuss the factorial function that returns an integer. If you consider a nonrecursive execution, it is possible to use an iterative method, and the subprogram is as follows:

```c
int iterativeFactorial (int n) {
int i, fatt;
fatt = 1;
   if (n>1){
      for (i = 1; i <=n; i++){
         fatt = fatt * i;
      }
   }
return fatt;
}
```

In the other case, a recursive method is used.

```c
int recursiveFactorial (int n) {
int fatt;
```

129

```c
if (n == 0 || n == 1) fatt = 1;
else {
    int nn=n-1;
    fatt = n * recursiveFactorial (nn);
}
```

In the program, first variables and function prototypes are defined, and then the two methods are called.

Source Program and Program Output

The C code is shown here:

```c
#include <stdio.h>
    int n, fattIterative, fattRecursive;
    int iterativeFactorial (int n) ;
    int recursiveFactorial (int n);

    main() {
     printf("Insert n: ");
     scanf("%d",&n);
     fattIterative = iterativeFactorial (n);
     fattRecursive = recursiveFactorial (n);
     printf("Iterative factorial: %d \n", fattIterative);
     printf("Recursive factorial: %d ", fattRecursive);
  }

int iterativeFactorial (int n) {
int i, fatt;
fatt = 1;
    if (n>1){
       for (i = 1; i <=n; i++){
          fatt = fatt * i;
       }
    }
```

```c
return fatt;
}

int recursiveFactorial (int n) {
int fatt;

if (n == 0 || n == 1) fatt = 1;
else {
    int nn=n-1;
    fatt = n * recursiveFactorial (nn);
}

return fatt;
}
```

Figure 3-29 shows the program output.

```
Insert n: 5
Iterative factorial: 120
Recursive factorial: 120
```

Figure 3-29. *Recursive and iterative factorial output*

Recursive Algorithm: Fibonacci Sequence

For the calculation of Fibonacci numbers, now we will try to find the n-th number in the Fibonacci series with the most efficient algorithm.

We are interested in the following:

- Finding the result of a problem that is correct and as simple as possible

- Finding the result of a problem that is as efficient as possible in terms of execution time and memory

A First Method

If one considers the recursive development, the subprogram for the algorithm is as follows:

```
int fibonacciRicorsivo(int n)
{
  if (n == 0) return 0;
  if (n<= 2) return 1;
  else return fibonacciRicorsivo [n-1] +
                      fibonacciRicorsivo [n-2];
}
```

Second Method

Now, we have to make an important consideration: we do not need the entire sequence, but just the *n-th* value! Therefore, the recursive algorithm for the Fibonacci calculation is slow, as it continues to calculate repeatedly the solution of the same subproblem.

Therefore, we can try to store in an array the solutions of the subproblems. The new algorithm is as follows:

```
algorithm fibonacciArray(int n) → int
    if Fib is an array of integer
    Fib[1] ← Fib[2] ← 1
    for i = 3 to n do
        Fib[i] ← Fib[i-1] + Fib[i-2]
    return Fib[n]
```

If you consider nonrecursive development, the subprogram for the algorithm is the following:

```
int  fibonacciVettore (int n)    {
    int fibonacci [M];
    int i;

    fibonacci [1]=1;
    fibonacci [2]=1;

    for (i = 3; i<= n ;i++)
      fibonacci [i] = fibonacci [i-1] + fibonacci [i-2];

    return fibonacci [n];
}
```

Third Method

In the previous case, the algorithm is faster than the first one. From a computational point of view, however, it continues to occupy unnecessary memory because we do not need to store all the Fibonacci numbers. Therefore, we can get the last two numbers from two variables whose values are given by the sum of the previous ones. Why not save time by using two variables of the previous solutions? We can create a loop by storing only the last two values in two variables.

Therefore, let's just try to store the last two values in two variables. The new algorithm is as follows:

```
algorithm fibonacciVar(int n) → int
    a ← b ← 1
    for i = 3 to n do
        c ← a+b
        a ← b
        b ← c
    return b
```

If you consider nonrecursive development, storing only the last two variables of interest, the subprogram for the algorithm is as follows:

```
int  fibonacciVariabili (int n)   {
    int i,a,b,c;
    a=1;
    b=1;
        for (i = 3; i<= n ;i++)
        {
            c = a+ b;
            a = b;
            b=c;
        }
    return b;
 }
```

An Introduction to Algorithmic Complexity

In this section, we'll introduce the algorithmic complexity in the previous example. Intuitively, it is possible to say that the iterative solution that stores the previous two values is the one that provides the optimum compromise between use of memory and number of operations.

However, which algorithm is better? Is it possible to identify a method that allows us to "measure" which solution is better than another?

We could use as an indicator the number of operations it performs to get a result. In that case, we would need to count only the most important operations that a program executes and that are significant for the solution of the problem.

In this case, we can choose to calculate the computational cost of an algorithm, evaluating the computational cost of the following operations:

- **Assignment or simple instructions (sum, increase, decrease, etc.)**: The computational cost = 1.

- **Compound statements**: The computational cost = the sum of all simple instructions.

- **Test instructions**: The computational cost = the sum of the cost of the longest instructions added to the cost of the test instruction.

- **Loop statements**: The computational cost = the sum of the cost of the instructions in the loop added to the cost of the test instruction. Finally, this sum must be multiplied by the number of cycles of the loop.

Table 3-1 shows the result (relative to the code developed in the next paragraph).

Table 3-1. *Fibonacci Algorithmic Complexity*

Value (IN)/Fibonacci (OUT)	Recursive Code	Iterative Code with an Array	Iterative Code with Variables
2	Instructions 1	Instructions 1	Instructions 1
1	Assignments 1	Assignments 1	Assignments 1
3	Instructions 4	Instructions 2	Instructions 2
2	Assignments 3	Assignments 7	Assignments 9
4	Instructions 7	Instructions 3	Instructions 3
3	Assignments 5	Assignments 10	Assignments 14

(*continued*)

Table 3-1. (*continued*)

Value (IN)/Fibonacci (OUT)	Recursive Code	Iterative Code with an Array	Iterative Code with Variables
5 5	Instructions 13 Assignments 9	Instructions 4 Assignments 13	Instructions 4 Assignments 19
18 2584	Instructions 7750 Assignments 5167	Instructions 17 Assignments 36	Instructions 17 Assignments 84
30 832040	Instructions 2496118 Assignments 1664079	Instructions 29 Assignments 88	Instructions 29 Assignments 144

Note that the winning algorithms are the last two. They are almost aligned in computational cost (the third algorithm uses more operations than the second to allow the switch of the variables). Considering the occupation of memory and the scope of the problem, you can claim to have found the best result.

Source Program and Program Output

The C code is shown next. Additional variables have been introduced to evaluate the computational cost of each algorithm.

```c
#include <stdio.h>
int num, fibRecursive, fibArray, fibVariable;
int n_instruction, n_assignment;
int fibonacciRecursive (int n) ;
int fibonacciArray (int n);
int fibonacciVariable (int n);
```

```c
main() {
  printf("Insert number: ");
  scanf("%d",&num);

n_instruction = 0;
n_assignment = 0;
fibRecursive = fibonacciRecursive (num);
printf("\nFibonacci number recursive: %d \n", fibRecursive);
printf("n_instruction: %d \n", n_instruction);
printf("n_assignment: %d \n", n_assignment);

n_instruction = 0;
n_assignment = 0;
fibArray = fibonacciArray (num);
printf("\nFibonacci number with array: %d \n", fibArray);
printf("n_instruction: %d \n", n_instruction);
printf("n_assignment: %d \n", n_assignment);

n_instruction = 0;
n_assignment = 0;
fibVariable = fibonacciVariable (num);
printf("\nFibonacci number with variable: %d \n", fibVariable);
printf("n_instruction: %d \n", n_instruction);
printf("n_assignment: %d \n", n_assignment);

  }

int fibonacciRecursive(int n)
{
int fibonacci;

//test instruction
n_instruction++;
if (n<= 2) {
```

```c
    //one assignment
    n_assignment++;
    fibonacci=1;
}
else {
    // one assignment
    n_assignment++;
    //a sum
    n_instruction++;
    fibonacci= fibonacciRecursive(n-1) + fibonacciRecursive (n-2);
}
return fibonacci;
}

int  fibonacciArray (int n)    {
  int fibonacci;
  int fibonacciArr[100];
  int i;

  if (n==1){
   //test instruction
   n_instruction++;
   //one assignment
   n_assignment++;
   fibonacci =1;
  }

  if (n==2){
   //test instruction
   n_instruction++;
   //one assignment
   n_assignment++;
```

```
   fibonacci =1;
  }

  if (n>2){
  //test instruction
  n_instruction++;
  //three assignment: i=3; fibonacci [2]=1; fibonacci [1]=1
  n_assignment=n_assignment+3;
  fibonacciArr [1]=1;
  fibonacciArr [2]=1;

  for (i = 3; i<= n ;i++)   {
       //increment of index i and final test
       n_assignment=n_assignment+2;

         //a sum
       n_instruction++;

       //one assignment
       n_assignment++;

             fibonacciArr [i] = fibonacciArr [i-1] +
             fibonacciArr [i-2];
      }
        //one assignment
       n_assignment++;
       fibonacci=   fibonacciArr [n];
  }
 return fibonacci ;
}

int  fibonacciVariable (int n)   {
  int i,a,b,c;
  int fibonacci;
```

```c
if (n==1){
 //test instruction
 n_instruction++;
 //one assignment
 n_assignment++;
 fibonacci =1;
}

if (n==2){
 //test instruction
 n_instruction++;
 //one assignment
 n_assignment++;
 fibonacci =1;
}

if (n>2){
//test instruction
n_instruction++;
//three assignment: i=3; a=1; b=1
n_assignment=n_assignment+3;
a=1;
b=1;

    for (i = 3; i<= n ;i++)
    {
    //increment of index i and final test
      n_assignment=n_assignment+2;

        c = a+ b;
        a = b;
        b=c;
        //a sum
```

```
            n_instruction++;
            //three assignment for the switch
            n_assignment= n_assignment+3;
        }
        //one assignment
        n_assignment++;
        fibonacci=c;
    }
    return fibonacci;
}
```

Figure 3-30 shows the program output.

```
Insert number: 8

Fibonacci number recursive: 21
n_instruction: 61
n_assignment: 41

Fibonacci number with array: 21
n_instruction: 7
n_assignment: 22

Fibonacci number with variable: 21
n_instruction: 7
n_assignment: 34
```

Figure 3-30. *Fibonacci output of the three methods*

Index

A

Algorithm
    defined, 13
    flow chart, 15
    natural language, 16
Algorithmic complexity
    C code, Fibonacci,
        136, 138, 139, 141
    computational cost, 135
    Fibonacci, 135, 136, 141
    indicator, 134
Arithmetic operators, 73
Array exercise, 30–32, 94–96
    C code, 93, 94
    flow chart, 27, 28
    load inputs, 28, 29
    loops types, 92
    output, 94
Arrays, 5, 6, 72

B

Binary search, 104–107
    failure values, 46
    flow chart, 43, 44
    search key, 43, 45
    sublist, 41
Bottom-up approach, 14, 15

Bubble sort, 47–51, 107–109
    defined, 47
    flow chart, 48
    iterations, 50
    swapping, 47, 49
Business Process Model and
        Notation (BPMN), 16

C

Code fundamentals
    Boolean type, 73
    functions, 74, 75
    fundamental or primitive
        types, 71
    library functions, 75
    main() command, 70
    statements, 76–79
    variable declaration, 73
    type void, 72

D, E

Data structure, 1–12
Decimal to binary number
        conversion
    algorithm steps, 33
    C code, 98, 99
    DIV function, 33
    example, 34

© Luciano Manelli 2020
L. Manelli, *Introducing Algorithms in C*, https://doi.org/10.1007/978-1-4842-5623-7

Printed in the United States
By Bookmasters